Personal Power Books
(in 12 volumes), Vol. XII

Regenerative Power
or Vital Rejuvenation

WILLIAM WALKER ATKINSON
EDWARD E. BEALS

COSIMOCLASSICS

NEW YORK

"Nature has been very careful to provide for
that attraction between the sexes in the animal kingdom
which will cause them to frequent the society of each
other, particularly during the mating season. Ever among
the animals, such as the fishes, and the frogs, where the
male-element is deposited upon the eggs after they are
laid by the female, there is manifested a strong
sex-companionship between the two sexes
during this period."

—from Chapter II, The Power of Sex

CONTENTS

REGENERATIVE POWER

I

REGENERATION

In this book we shall present for your consideration certain facts and principles concerning the conservation and the efficient employment of the Life Forces or Vital Force generally known as Vitality, or rather of certain of its subtle forms. This instruction proceeds along lines which are not generally recognized by or known to the average individual, although the facts and principles in question were known to the ancient sages, and have been taught and practiced for many centuries by many persons who have had the benefit of this ancient wisdom which was formerly the exclusive property of the secret schools of esoteric philosophy in Oriental lands and in ancient Greece.

This knowledge also was imparted thousands of years ago by the great Hindu sages to their chosen pupils, and formed a part of the occult instruction given to the student of the Inner Teaching of the Brahmans and Buddhists of that land. There is every reason to believe that a similar teaching was given the neophytes in the occult schools of ancient Persia, Chaldea, and Egypt. References to it are also found in the esoteric writings of the ancient Hebrews. It was taught in "The Mysteries" of the arcane schools of ancient Greece, and was taken over from this source by the Neoplatonists, and the Gnostics of the early centuries of the Christian Era. It was also a part of the teaching of the Essenes, that strange school of esoteric wisdom which is believed to have exerted a strong influence upon the early Christian Church.

But here, as in many other instances, the knowledge which originally was held to be based upon the existence and activity of certain hidden and secret forces of Nature, or perhaps even upon actual supernatural powers, is now known to be but a scientific statement of purely natural cause and effect arising from the power and activity of simple, elemental forces of Nature which always have existed and have been operative, but which have been comparatively unknown to the great masses of people. Science has dispelled much of the mystery of the ancient philosophies and religions, but it has served also to corroborate their original facts.

Thus, Electricity and Magnetism, long known to the ancients and ascribed by them to supernatural causes, have been brought under the authority of Natural Law, and then harnessed and made to work efficiently in the service of man. Likewise, for many centuries the phenomena of Mental Influence were known to the ancients, and ascribed by them to occult and supernatural causes. Modern Science was at first disposed to deny such phenomena, and to regard the whole belief as pure superstition. However, in time their true causes were discovered, and the subjects of Hypnotism and Mental Suggestion is now taught in the highest schools, and is given a place in all of the authoritative textbooks.

So it has been, and is, with this phase or form of Vital Power or Life Force which constitutes the subject of our present consideration. For many centuries, and in many lands, it formed a part of the esoteric instruction in the secret schools of the occult philosophies, and in the temples of the ancient religions. Its principles of application were discovered, and methods for their employment were evolved. It was taught only to the chosen few, being regarded as a precious secret to be withheld from the masses and to be reserved for the elect. It was believed to be supernatural in origin and nature, and was treated with an almost religious awe and veneration; in fact, in many cases it formed a part of the inner and higher religious teachings of the priesthood, from which the laity were debarred.

Later, it formed a part of the secret and occult doctrines which were held and taught by the arcane schools of philosophy in the Middle Ages, traces of which are now found in the rituals of many of the modern secret orders and societies, though their real meaning and spirit has been lost and only the verbal outer covering or shell remains. It was this knowledge which was the real and true underlying reason for the advocacy of celibacy in the priesthoods and holy orders of many religions, including those of the Early Christian Church. It was this knowledge which was the animating spirit of the early schools and orders of asceticism, which afterward developed into fanatical phases and forms, the true spirit and meaning of the teaching having been lost.

Modern Science, true to its customary procedure, for a long time was disposed to regard this ancient teaching as fantastic superstition, ignorance, and supernaturalism, and to deny to it any virtue or validity. However, in time the physiologists discovered the existence and activity of certain principles concerned with the reproductive organism, and with its effect and action upon the entire physical and mental system of the individual. The investigations and observations of the effect of certain glands of the body upon general health and vigor gave new interest to the subject, and certain recent experiments along the lines of gland transplantation have revealed marvelous results.

There is every indication that the present century is destined to witness many important discoveries along these particular lines. However, it is not necessary to wait for these anticipated discoveries in order to benefit by what is already known to careful thinkers concerning this subject. While such discoveries may be regarded by some as necessary before the seal of authority of Science may be formally placed upon the general principles and facts concerned with the general subject nevertheless there are thousands of careful investigators and conservative thinkers who feel that sufficient is already known concerning these facts and principles to justify their being accepted as a basis for theory and practice by all persons of average intelligence. Such individuals have long known of these facts and principles, and have had practical demonstrations of their value to mankind when properly and intelligently applied.

The essence and spirit of this body of knowledge, principle and mass of facts, is indicated by the term "Regeneration" employed with a special meaning and content. We ask you to consider carefully this term in such special meaning, to the end that you may "catch the spirit" of the idea and principle embodied in it. As we have sought to impress upon you in other volumes of this series, it is always well to begin with a clear understanding of the principal terms employed in a discussion, argu- ment, or presentation of a proposition or prin- ciple—to know "just what" is being consid- ered and discussed. So many terms are em- ployed with so many different shades of mean- ing, and often with forms of meaning quite op- posed to each other, that it is always proper to investigate a term employed in a particular sense, in order to ascertain "just what" is sought to be indicated by it, and is involved in its content.

The term "Regeneration," of course, is de- rived from the term "Generation." The prefix "re" means "again," "anew," etc. The term "Generation" means "the act, process, or re- sult of generating," and is derived from the verb "to generate." The term "Generate" means: "To beget, to produce, to engender, to cause to be, to bring into life; to originate, especially by means of a vital or chemical pro- cess." It is usually employed in the sense of "begetting," "reproduction," or "procreation," or the production of the young of animal or plant life.

"Regeneration" is defined as: "The act of regenerating, or of generating or producing anew; and, in a special sense, of "giving new life, strength, or vigor to a living being." A person is said to be "regenerated" physically when by any means or method he acquires "new life, new energy, new vigor." The theologians, recognizing the strength of the word, employed it more or less figuratively in the sense of: "Being born anew in spirit"; in such usage the term is frequently employed in theological expression and religious teaching. This theological usage, however, is noted here merely for the purpose of general statement: our present employment of the term has no reference whatever to such special usage and meaning.

In the special meaning of the term "Regeneration," which has grown around it in the course of thought along the lines of our subject, the "giving of new life, strength, or vigor" to the individual is literally true, and not merely figurative. By means of such Regeneration, the individual is given continued new life, strength, and vigor—mental as well as physical. Just as every living thing has been given original life, strength, and vigor by Generation, so may it be given new life, strength, and vigor by Regeneration. In both Generation and Regeneration, moreover, the same potent forces of Nature are involved and set into activity, i.e., the forces concerned with the sexual or reproductive organism.

The "secret doctrine," "inner teaching," "arcane wisdom," etc., of the ancient philosophies

and religions, and of the more modern secret
societies and schools, concerning the secret of
Regeneration, is this: "Nature's Generative
Power may be employed as Regenerative Power; the same forces which bring man into life,
strength, and vigor, will renew and reproduce
his life, strength, and vigor, if rightly applied
and directed."

This is a somewhat startling doctrine when
announced for the first time to the average individual. To him it seems contrary to common sense and opposed to common experience.
It is only when he begins to understand the
basic principles of the idea, and when the misconceptions concerning it have been removed
by explanation, that the light begins to dawn
upon him.   When he has fully grasped the
fundamental principles, and the essential reasoning involved in the idea, he tends toward
becoming quite enthusiastic concerning it, and
to him it seems self-evident. The more he con-
siders it, the more reasonable and certain does
it become; and when he learns of the discoveries of modern Science concerning it, he passes beyond the point of possible doubt or distrust.

Before presenting to you the conclusions of
advanced modern scientific thought concerning
this subject of Regeneration, we shall ask you
to undertake a general, brief and cursory consideration of the history of this idea of Regen-

eration as it was conceived by the ancient philosophers and sages. This, not only because of the general interest connected with such consideration, but also that hereafter you may recognize the hidden and cryptic references to Regeneration which appear in many of the old mystic, occult and esoteric writings and formulas—among those of alchemy as well as those of mysticism. An understanding of this will throw light on many hitherto dark subjects, and will prove the key which will unlock the doors of many old and strange doctrines. In the light of modern knowledge, many of these old presentations of occult knowledge may be read and studied with profit; but without this light, they will ever remain dark subjects to the modern student.

The attention of the ancient thinkers was directed from the very first to the Mystery of Reproduction—the Miracle of Generation. Observing the operations of its laws in plant and animal life, and noting that the Essence of Life seemed to be concentrated into the tiny seed of the plant or the animal, they soon came to realize that Nature here manifested a marvelous power of concentration of the Life Forces into a small space. Consequently they regarded such concentrated Vital Force with a religious awe, and considered it to be supernatural.

Further observations concerning the effect of sexual mutilation upon animals and men, and of the changes wrought in mind and body by the quickening of the reproductive power in puberty and adolescence, and by the decrease of such power in old age, led these ancient thinkers to the conclusion that in the generative forces were to be found a highly concentrated Essence of Life which, if properly controlled and directed, was capable of renewing and continuing the vital strength and vigor of the individual almost indefinitely.

In the very ancient Yoga Philosophy of the Hindus, dating back to long before the Christian Era, are found many references to this control and application of this Regenerative Power, i.e., of the Generative Power employed for the purpose of increasing and maintaining the mental and physical energy, strength and vigor of the individual, in addition to its more familiar offices and activities. Ths Regenerative Power was known as the "Ojas," and was conceived as of a fiery, ardent, highly concentrated and highly active nature. It was taught that by means of the direction of the Ojas along certain physical and psychical channels not only might the Yogi greatly increase his physical strength, energy and vigor, but that he might also thereby cultivate great mental powers and psychic qualities.

Swami Vivekananda, the celebrated Hindu teacher who visited Europe and America about thirty years ago, and who taught Yoga to

western students for several years, says of this
Ojas Force in his book entitled "Raja Yoga":

"The Yogis claim that of all the energies
that the human body comprises, the highest is
that what they call Ojas. Now this Ojas is
stored up in the brain, and the more the Ojas
is in a man's head, the more powerful he is, the
more intellectual, the more spiritually strong
will that man be. This is the action of Ojas.
One man may speak beautiful language and
beautiful thoughts, but they do not impress
people; another man speaks neither beautiful
language nor beautiful thoughts, yet his words
charm. That is the power of Ojas coming
out. Every movement coming from him will
be powerful. Now in mankind there is more
or less of this Ojas stored up. And all the
forces that are working in the body, in their
highest form, become Ojas. You must remember that it is only a question of transformation. The same force which is working outside, as electricity or magnetism, will become
changed into inner force; the same forces that
are working as muscular energy will be
changed into Ojas.

"The Yogis say that that part of the human
energy which is expressed as sex energy, in
sexual functions, sexual thought, and so on,
when checked and controlled, easily becomes
changed into Ojas; and as this lowest centre
is the one which guides all these functions,

therefore the Yogi pays particular attention to
that centre. He tries to take up all this sexual
energy and convert it into Ojas. It is only
the chaste man or woman who can make the
Ojas rise and become stored in the brain, and
that is why chastity has always been considered the highest virtue, because man feels that
if he is unchaste, spirituality goes away; he
loses mental vigor, and strong moral stamina.
That is why in all of the religious orders in
the world that have produced spiritual giants
you will always find this intense chastity insisted upon. That is why the monks came into
existence, giving up marriage. There must be
perfect chastity, in thought, word and deed.
Without it the practice of Raja Yoga is dangerous, and may lead to insanity. If people
practice Raja Yoga and at the same time lead
an impure life, how can they expect to become
Yogis?"

The above is not merely the personal teaching of Vivekananda: it is his statement of the
teaching of the Yoga Philosophy which was
established several thousand years ago—long
before our present era. Its essential idea is
found to permeate many of the modern Hindu
philosophies and religions, though in many
cases it has become corrupted by the loss of its
original spirit, and has developed into fanatical
asceticism and a degredation of the idea of sex
and reproduction. The original idea of the

teaching was that sex is not impure, but that in their proper place and use its activities are proper and normal; but that in its perverted excesses and misuse it becomes an evil. Regeneration is upheld, not because Generation is wrong, but because Regeneration is an additional field for the expression and manifestatin of the concentrated Vital Force present in the system of man.

The ancient Buddhists also held that Regeneration was a function and office of the Creative Powers present in the sexual organism. They held that the Will-to-Live, that Active Principle which is the Cause of Creation, exists in its most concentrated and potent form in the Sexual Energy; and that the latter may be employed not only in Generation, but also in Regeneration. This Regeneration, they taught, produces great mental and spiritual strength, energy and vigor, which if directed intelligently will develop even supernormal powers of mind and body in the individual. They held, in some cases, that this Creative Energy, or Will-to-Live, would carry the individual beyond the necessity of physical life in reincarnated forms, and would deliver him from the Wheel of Life and thereby enable him to reach Nirvana.

The ancient Egyptians also taught a similar doctrine in the esoteric and secret Isis cult. The Creative Principle, or Life-Energy, was

conceived as feminine. The neophyte was
taught that by a conservation of this Life-Energy, and a refusal to expend it in Generation,
it might be transmuted into Vital Force which ,
by the process of Regeneration would vitalize,
animate and vivify the body and mind of the
person, and give to him psychical and spiritual
powers which are surely superhuman and pos-
sibly supernatural as well. This teaching was
withheld from the common people, being reserved for the elect. It was held that in certain cases the mortal man might even be transformed into a god by means of the efficient
employment of the Power of Regeneration.

The ancient Jews, in their esoteric teachings
and doctrines, held to the truth of a similar belief and practice. Constant references to it are
found in the Kaballah, and in other occult He-
brew writings. Some of these ancient writers
taught that the story of Adam and Eve is
merely an allegorical representation of this
principle. This theory held that Adam and
Eve represented the male and female human
beings as they were originally; these beings
were destined to live forever, their Creative
Energy being constantly turned inward in the
processes of Regeneration. They were tempted
by the suggestions of an Evil Spirit, and thereafter turned their Creative Energy into the
channels of Generation and away from those
of Regeneration, thereby perpetuating the race

as a whole but bringing Death to its individual members.

The Neoplatonists, and the Gnostics, two great schools of mystical philosophy which flourished in the early centuries of the Christian Era, taught the Doctrine of Regeneration in various forms, and many of the members of the Early Christian Church were influenced by it. These schools obtained their teaching from both Oriental and Ancient Greek sources—the ancient Greek Mysteries included teaching and practice of Regeneration. Gradually, however, the spirit of the teaching was lost, and all that was left was the pitiful husk of perverted Asceticism, and a Degradation of the Sexual Ideals. Sex grew to be considered unclean; repression, and ascetism became gloried as holy. The influence of this perversion and misapplication of the original teaching and doctrine is felt even unto this day.

In the Middle Ages the alchemists and occult philosophers devoted much attention to the subject of Regeneration. Frequent references to it under the figurative term, "The Elixir of Life," are found in old writings of these thinkers. Legends inform us that some of these ancients' developed the power and ability to live far beyond the allotted lifetime of man, and retained their full vigor, strength and vital energies to the last. The masses of people thought that the "Elixir of Life" was

a cordial or tincture of wonderful properties;
but those who knew the secret code realized
that this potent Elixir was naught but the
highly concentrated Creative Energies of man,
existing in potency and latency in his reproductive organism, the same being transmuted
into an Inner Vitality instead of being dissipated in lustful practices or expended in the
functions of Generation.

In this fundamental idea of Regeneration,
then, is to be found the true explanation of the
universal insistence upon chastity, continence,
and often upon celibacy, on the part of the
priests and great spiritual leaders, as well as
on the part of the great occultists and partak-
ers of "the Mysteries." This was not, as generally supposed, because of any idea of the essential impurity of Sex, but rather because of
the belief that the higher powers of man,
physical, mental, psychical and spiritual, were
increased in power and efficiency by means of
the practice of Regeneration rather than that
of Generation—the turning of the Creative Energy inward, rather than outward. It was the
idea of Creation on the mental, psychical and
spiritual planes, rather than upon the plane of
materiality and the physical, that was back of
this common custom and rule. But, as we have
said, the spirit of the idea was frequently lost
in the passage of the years, and only the ugly,
lifeless, outer shell remained.

Modern Science has now discovered certain remarkable facts in the realm of physiology which tend to prove the correctness of the old doctrine of Transmutation of Sexual Energy, or Regeneration. More than this, actual surgical experiments have demonstrated that the theory can be made to work out in practice, in the case of animals and of human beings as well. Of course, new theories are being advanced to explain these phenomena, and new names are being coined to apply to them. But the old principle and essential facts remain the same, as true now under the new theories and new names as they were under the old theories and ancient terminology.

In our present consideration of this interesting and important subject we shall take the best to be found in either, and both, the ancient and the modern teachings and knowledge concerning the facts and the principles involved therein. There is an essential and fundamental agreement between them, underlying the differences of theory and interpretation, and despite the character of the different terms employed to indicate the phenomena and the principle of which they are manifestations.

II

THE POWER OF SEX

The term "Sex," in its original and general meaning, is defined as: "The distinguishing peculiarity of male and female; or the distinction of the offices and functions of the male and female living individuals." In its later, and more special meaning, however, the term is employed in the sense of: "The functions and offices of the male and female living individuals which are concerned with the primary and secondary manifestations of the sexual or reproductive powers and activities."

Sex is an evolutionary manifestation of Nature. It has as its evident primary purpose and intent the furthering of the work of reproduction of the living forms which have been produced by Nature, or by those of her processes which are known as "The Life Forces," or "The Vital Energies," and which are concerned with the maintenance, preservation and continuance of Life in the forms which have been evolved as the vehicles or mechanism of the manifestation of Life.

Nature, in those phases or forms of her manifestations which are concerned with Life, evidently has as her primary purpose the production and maintenance of the life-forms. To these ends she devotes an enormous amount and a high degree of energy, force and power, and manifests an almost incredible degree of activity. Whatever Nature is held to be at the last, and whatever else may be conceived to be a part of her purposes and designs, it cannot be denied that she seems to be intensely concerned and indefatigably active in the direction of creating, preserving and continuing Life in and through the life-forms which she has produced in the processes of evolution.

To this end, she has evolved and perfected the wondrous physical mechanism by means of which the physical processes are carried on. To this end, she has developed the recuperative and reparative agencies in the organism of the living creature by means of which are overcome the harmful effects of injuries and disease. To this end, she has quickened the senses, instinct, and reasoning powers of the living creature, that these may be employed for the preservation of the physical organism through which Life manifests itself. Finally, to this end she has evolved the marvelous mechanism of the reproductive organism by means of which the living creature is enabled to perpetuate, reproduce and generate its kind; this being accompanied by the marvelous physical, mental and emotional characteristics which have been evolved in order to serve this purpose and to promote its ends.

The ancient Buddhists recognized this tendency in Nature which acts in the direction of promoting Life and living. In their teaching concerning "The Will-to-Live" they claimed that all Creation proceeds from and by means of this primal desire and impulse. Schopenhauer taught a similar doctrine. In his philosophy, the "kernel of things" is this urge, striving, seeking, desire or "will-to-live." Both the Buddhists and Schopenhauer also held that this "will-to-live" has its most active form in the Sex Instinct, or Reproductive Urge. Bergson, in his modern philosophy, holds that the Vital Impulse is the essential and fundamental energy, power, or force manifested in the universal activities.

Nature, however, seems to have changed her mind, or else to have improved upon her original plans, in this matter of the continuance of Life in her living forms. It would seem that from the very first, however, she found herself under the Law of Change, and that by reason of this she was either unable, or else not desirous of, continuing the existence of the living creature permanently in its original form. At any rate, there seems to have been an inherent desire and tendency toward change and variation in the life-forms— the processes of Evolution seem to establish

this fact—whatever may be its real reason or
cause. It was apparently in the manifestation
of this evident intent, purpose, tendency, or
necessity, that Nature evolved Sex in living-
forms.

Those who have not studied the subject are
generally of the belief that the distinction of
Sex is manifest in all the living forms, even
among the lowest and most elemental forms.
But this is not correct; the distinction of Sex
was absent in the first manifestations of Life,
and was not evolved until the processes of
Creative Evolution had proceeded comparatively far in the scale of Life. The lowest and
most elemental life-forms of course were possessed of the power of Reproduction or Generation—this, indeed, is one of the most essential
of the characteristics of plant-life and animal-
life. But the distinctions of Sex were not present in the elementary life-forms of the past,
nor in the existing primitive life-forms. Nature managed to proceed without the distinction of "male" and "female" for a considerable
time—though it may be asserted that if Sex
and Reproductive Power are identical, then
Sex was present from the first, though without
the differentation of male and female qualities.

The simplest and most elementary life-forms
are those of the single-cell creatures which are
found in the slime of the ocean beds. These
forms are very minute, and are of such extreme

simplicity of organization that they are not, strictly speaking, organisms at all—for they are not possessed of true organs. They resemble minute globules of gelatinous substance, very much like glue. Yet they perform the processes of assimilation and digestion of food and of its elimination; also those of reproduction.

These lowly life-forms do not manifest the differentation of male and female sex-characteristics. According to which viewpoint we adopt, we may state that they are either (a) without Sex, or (b) are all female, or (c) are bi-sexual, i.e., a combination of both sexes. These elementary creatures reproduce their kind, just as truly as do the highest species of plant-life or animal-life. But they reproduce themselves in a very primitive manner, namely, by division or separation.

The elementary parent creature grows in size, and finally assumes the appearance of a miniature dumb-bell, with two swollen ends connected by a tiny, thin filament or connecting-rod. Finally, this filament or connecting-rod breaks, and there exist two living creatures where before there was but one. It has been said that if these creatures were possessed of reason, each would be unable to decide whether it was the mother or the daughter—the parent or the offspring. So far as Science has been able to determine, there is present in this

reproductive process no union of cell-elements,
no conjugation of reproductive factors. The
creature is but a single cell, and no differentation of sexual elements has been discovered to
exist in it.

A little higher in the scale of elementary
life-forms we find that division of the animal
kingdom called the Protozoa. These tiny creatures are also but single-celled individuals, but
in many cases these unite into groups and
form a compound organism. These creatures
also reproduce by subdivision, or separation,
similar to that above noted; but before this
subdivision or separation takes place there occurs what is known as sexual "conjugation," in
which two single-celled creatures unite and
coalesce; and when the subdivision begins
there appear on the parent form a number of
tiny "buds," the latter afterward dropping off
and thereafter existing as separate individuals.
These uniting and coalescing two cells, however, are not true male and female; instead,
they are bi-sexual, and the male element of
each fertilizes the female element of the other,
or, more technically stated, "the male elements
of the two individuals are exchanged, and the
new male nucleus fuses with the original female portion of each"; the two reorganized individual cells separate from each other after
the conjugation, and "reassume their original

existence before beginning again to divide in the usual manner."

Here, then, we see the differentation of male and female—the Evolution of Sex, in the strict meaning of the latter term. "Why," we may ask, "does Nature make this change; why did she not continue to reproduce by simple subdivision and separation of the creature?" Science answers: "The Origin of Sex is an unsettled problem. We do not understand how or why, from being at first hermaphroditic or asexual, as was probably the case, the male and female characteristics became gradually established."

On the other hand, Science perceives that Variation proceeds from Sex differentation, and as Variation seems to be the trend of Nature, this may be the "reason" for the evolution of Sex. The following quotation from an authoritative reference work points to this conclusion: "The male is the more active, more variable, and specialized sex, while the female is passive, conservative, and departs less from the normal standard. It would be a natural result that the offspring would tend to vary. Weissmann goes so far as to claim that the intermingling of the sexual elements in fertilization is the only cause of variation. Before him, Treviranus, Brooks, and Galton claimed that the sexual reproduction provokes variation."

In the evolution of the differentation of Sex

—the distinction between male and female creatures, cells, or elements—there was produced (1) the male creature, cell, or element, distinguished by the presence of "sperm" in the normal adult creature, cell, or element; and (2) the female creature, cell, or element, distinguished by the presence of "ova" or eggs in the normal adult creature, cell, or element. An organism producing "sperm" is male; one producing "ova" is a female; and one producing both "sperm" and "ova" is a true hermaphrodite; while one producing neither "sperm" or "ova" is a neuter—though neuters are, for the most part, incomplete females.

But Nature, even after evolving and producing the differentation of the male and female elements of reproduction, did not at once begin to place these elements, separated, in different individuals—it did not at once begin to manifest male and female forms. Rather, it seemingly was at first inclined to place both elements in one life-form, thus rendering each creature bi-sexual or hermaphroditic. Indeed, it extended this plan in some cases quite high up in the scale of the life-forms. For instance, it is quite common in plant-life; and in animal-life it is found in the oyster, in shell-fish in general, in barnacles, in the tape-worm, in the earth-worm, and in the great family of snails.

Science entertains differing opinions concerning the procedure of the Evolution of Sex,

and the place in time and order in it occupied
by the bi-sexual condition or hermaphroditism. The following quotation from Geddes, an
authority on the subject, will show these di-·
vergent views in brief form. Geddes says:

"One view of the matter is that hermaphroditism was the primitive state among the mul-
ticellular animals, at least after the differentation of the sex-elements had been accomplished. In alternating rhythms, eggs and
sperms were produced. The organism was
alternately male and female. On this primitive hermaphroditism, there may be more or
less of a recapitulation in the life-history of the
organism.

"Gegenbaur states the common opinion in
the following cautious and terse words: 'The
hermaphrodite stage is the lower, and the condition of distinct sexes has been derived from
it. Unisexual differentation, by the reduction
of one kind of sexual apparatus, takes place at
very different stages in the development of the
organism; and often when the sexual organs
have attained a very high degree of differentation.' * * * Quite different is the view which
regards hermaphroditism as a secondary condition, derived from a primitive unisexuality.
Thus Pelseneer maintains that the study of
certain of the lower forms of life 'shows that
in these groups the separation of the sexes
preceded hermaphroditism; various cases in

other groups tending to show that this is true universally; and the same conclusion applies to plants. In certain groups, at least, hermaphroditism is grafted upon the female sex'."

Whatever may have been the precise order of the conditions of unisexuality and bi-sexuality, respectively, all investigation seems to show that in the beginning the female distinctive element was predominant, and, in a sense, really the original element. The male distinctive element seems to have been developed by evolutionary differentation. The female element is concerned primarily with the actual reproductive process, the male element serving rather to energize by fertilization the female element, and thus affording a greater possibility or probability of variation. Even in the hermaphroditic forms, moreover, the fertilization is effected by the conjugation of the two elements of different creatures, instances of self-fertilization being rare and always more or less abnormal. In the conjugation of the hermaphroditic creatures the male element of each fertilizes the female element of the other —the dual fertilization being simultaneous in most cases.

As the scale of life is ascended, the male element becomes more active and more highly developed, and more important. Placed in separated individuals, the male element becomes better adapted for fertilization of the

female element in the female creatures far removed in space from the females of the immediate family-group to which the male belongs,
and thus still greater variety becomes possible.
The male element, high or low in form, however, is always the subordinate reproductive
element, the female element or mother-element
being the original and the always-predominant
factor in the reproductive process. In short,
the female-element is the factor essentially
necessary for reproduction in any form of life,
while the male element is the factor evolved
for convenience in the reproductive processes.
The female-element brings into being the form
of the offspring, the male-element being at the
best an accessory.

Nature has devised and perfected many very
ingenious methods by means of which the
male, or fertilizing element of Sex is conveyed
to its female, or generative element. In both
plant-life and animal-life the most intricate and
delicate mechanism for this purpose has been
produced by Nature. In fact, Nature seems
to have devoted a very large portion of her
time and work for this particular purpose, thus
showing the importance of the reproductive
processes in her general economy. In many
cases, indeed, particularly in the lower forms
of life, it would almost seem that the office of
living is actually subordinated to that of reproducing life—that the living thing exists, not

so much for the purpose of its own livingness,
but rather for the purpose of transmitting the
life-impulses and the vital-processes to future
individuals of its species and class. The individual good is seemingly secondary to the good
of the species, class, general group, and, above
all, to that of Life itself.

In plant-life the male-element, the fertilizing
factor, is called the "pollen," a fine, microscopic
dust or powder. The female-element, or generative factor, is called the "ovule," a tiny egg-
cell. The fertilization of the female-element,
or ovule, is effected by placing upon it the
male-element, or pollen. This "placing" is
effected in many different ways. In many
cases the pollen is carried to the flower by the
passing winds, again sometimes by the flowing
stream. In most cases, however, the pollen is
carried by small insects, small birds, and even
by small animals like the snail.

Bees are active factors in the fertilization of
plants, and many plants depend upon them exclusively for this service. Other plants depend
upon particular insects, it being held that each
and every plant has its own favorite and most
appropriate species of insect for such purposes.
The shape of the sexual channels of each flower is especially formed so as to fit properly
around the body of the fertilizing insect, so
that the pollen is easily attached to the latter
and as easily brushed off so that it may reach

the ovules of other flowers. The plants attract these insects by means of sweet, honeylike fluids, and by bright colors and fragrant odors.

The flower of the plant is its sexual organism. The Calyx, or cup of the flower, covering its lower parts, and usually green in color, and the Corolla, or crown of the flower, composed of petals which are usually colored beautifully, are the outer sexual organism of the plant. In them are contained the Stamen, or male appendage containing the pollen, and also the Pistil, or female appendage containing the ovules. These details of the sexual organism of the plants have a direct correspondence to the similar organism of animal-life. The same principle is operative in both plant-life and animal-life, and the same general mechanism is provided for its processes.

The following quotation from Kellog illustrates the wonderful instinctive action of the plants manifested in the processes of fertilization:

"In many instances, the action of plants seems almost to be prompted by intelligence. At the proper moment, the Corolla contracts in such a way as to bring the Stamen nearer to the Stigma (the crown of the Pistil), or in contact with it, so as to procure fecundation. In some aquatic plants, the flowers elevate themselves above the surface of the water while the process of fecundation is effected, submerging themselves immediately afterward. Other very curious changes occur in flowers of different species during the reproductive act.

"The Stigma is observed to become moistened, and even to become slightly odorous. Often, too, it becomes congested with the juices of the plant, and sometimes even acquires an uncommon and most remarkable degree of contractibility. This is the case with the Stigma of the tulip and of one variety of the sensitive-plant. In these plants it is observed to occur not only after the application of the pollen to the Stigma, but also when excited by any other means of stimulation.

"The flowers of some plants, during and after fecundation, also show an increase of heat, in some cases so marked as to be readily detected with the thermometer. This is said to be especially the case with the Arum of Italy. In some plants in which the Pistil is longer than the Stamens, thus elevating the Stigma above the Anthers, the female appendage of the plant is often observed to bend over and depress itself, so as to come within reach of the Anthers (the pollen-sac of the Stamen)."

In animal-life, Nature has been even still more ingenious and painstaking in her provision for the ready fertilization of the female-element of the creature. Fertilization, in animal-life, is summed up by Geddes in the following stated three stages, viz., "(1) The process whereby the spermatozoa are brought into general proximity to the ova; (2) the approach of the spermatozoon to the ovum; (3) the fertilization in the strict sense—the orderly union of the two sex-nuclei. ...." The Spermatozoa (singlar, Spermatozoon) are microscopic, living cells which exist in great numbers in the Sperm, or male-element of reproduction. Only one Spermatozoon, however, succeeds in penetrating the Ovum, or female, element of reproduction—the others perish; Nature provides this great number of competing Spermatozoa, thereby rendering almost certain the success of one of their number.

Geddes, the leading authority on the subject, says: "The adaptations which secure that the sperms shall reach the ova are very varied. Sometimes it seems almost a matter of chance, for the sperms from adjacent males to be washed into the female, as in sponges and bivalves, with the nutritive water-currents. In other cases, especially well seen in most fishes, the female deposits her unfertilized ova in the water; the male follows and covers them with spermatozoa. Many may have watched from a bridge the female salmon ploughing along the gravelly river bed depositing her ova, careful to secure a suitable ground, yet not disturbing the already laid eggs of her neighbors. Meanwhile she is attended by her (frequently much smaller) mate, who deposits milt upon the ova.

"In the frog, again, the eggs are fertilized by the male just as they leave the body of his embraced mate. Or it may be that the sperms are lodged in special packets, which are taken up by the female in most of the newts, or which are surrounded by one of the male arms in many cuttle-fishes, or passed by one of the male spider's palps (i.e., 'feelers' attached to the mouth of certain insects and crustaceans) to the female receptacle. In the majority of animals, e.g., insects and the higher vertebrates, however, the sperms pass direct from the male to the female. Even here the history is very varied. They may pass into special receptacles, as in insects, to be used as occasion demands; or, in higher animals, they may with persistent motor energy work their way up the female ducts. There they may soon meet with and fertilize ova which have been liberated from the ovary; or they may persist for a long period, as in the case of certain animals, to be used thereafter; or they may eventually perish, unused.

"When the sperms have come, in any of these varied ways, in close proximity to the ovum, there is every reason to believe that a strong osmotic attraction is set up between the two kinds of elements. . . . . . The spermatozoa, which seem so well to deserve Rolph's

epithet of 'starved,' appear to be powerfully
drawn to the well-nourished ovum, and the
latter frequently rises to meet the sperm in a
small 'attractive cone.' Often, however, there
is an obstacle in the way of entrance in the
form of the egg-shell, which may be penetrable
only at one spot, well called the micropyle.
Dewitz has made the interesting observation
that round the egg-shells of the cockroach ova,
the sperms move in regular circles of ever-
varying orbit; and points out that thus, soon-
er or late, a sperm must hit upon an entrance.
He showed that this was a characteristic motion of these elements on smooth spheres, for
round empty egg-shells or on similar vesicles
they moved in an equally orderly and system-
atic fashion.

"The persistence with which the sperma-
toza often force their way to the ova makes it
impossible to doubt the reality of a strong
chemotactic attraction. One illustration may
suffice. According to Dr. Sadone's account of
the impregnation of the rotifer, Hydatina Sen-
ta, the spermatozoa of the male, which are injected into the body-cavity of the female, reach
the totally enclosed eggs by boring through
the thin membrane at a point where the mature
ova are situated—a process not known in any
other animals. The oval head of a spermatozoon was seen to attach itself to the membrane of the ovary, the tail continuing to make

lashing movements, the head was gradually forced through the membrane, and the tail followed, the whole process taking about ten minutes."

Nature has been very careful to provide for that attraction between the sexes in the animal kingdom which will cause them to frequent the society of each other, particularly during the mating season. Even among animals, such as the fishes, and the frogs, where the male-element is deposited upon the eggs after they are laid by the female, there is manifested a strong sex-companionship between the two sexes during this period. The ordinary association of the future parents during the mating season, among the mammals and birds particularly, is too well known to require comment.

In the case of a species of fluke known as Diplozoon, the two individuals, male and female, physically combine in an almost lifetime union. Again, in the Bilharzia, a parasitic tremantode, the male carries the female about with him in a "gynaecophoric tube" composed of folds of skin. Once more, in certain species of barnacles the female carries her mate around with her, safely and securely secreted in a ·pocket-like contrivance in her body; this mate is much smaller than the female, and was formerly mistaken for a parasite.

III

DERIVATIVE SEX ATTRIBUTES

In addition to the primary attributes or characteristics of Sex which you have considered in the preceding section of this book, there are certain secondary or derivative sexual attributes or characteristics which you are now asked to consider in the present section. By "derivative attributes" are meant those characteristic qualities which are not primary or original, but which are secondary, incidental and obtained by derivation, in short, those characteristic qualities which flow and proceed from the primary, original, and fundamental nature of the thing under consideration, which thing in the present instance is Sex.

First among the secondary or derivative characteristics or attributes of sex is that known as Sexual Dimorphism, or the distinction of form and physical appearance of the two sexes of certain species. An authoritative reference work contains the following reference to this subject:

"Sexual Dimorphism is due to the rise of secondary characters. Such features are the male lion's mane, the horns of the buck, the gay plumage which distinguishes the cock

from the hen, and the plumes, colored combs
and wattles, topknots, brilliant, conspicuous
bands and spots, spurs, and those markings or
new plumage especially developed during the
breeding season. Males tend among vertebrates to be larger, they lead the flock, guard
the females and young; in character they are
more jealous and pugnacious. This is the case
not only with mammals and birds, but with
reptiles and frogs. The vociferous cries in
Spring of frogs and toads are mainly from
male throats, the females being much less
noisy.

"Certain fishes, such as the salmon, during
the breeding ·season, are distinguished by
bright colors and ornamental appendages. Of
the invertebrates only insects, spiders, and
crustacea afford examples. Among coleoptera
the stag-beetles are remarkable for their size
and the enormous jaws and horns of the males;
and there are two sets of males, those which
in lack of armature resemble the females, and
those which are much larger and remarkably
aberrant (i.e, deviating from type). In certain spiders the males are gayly colored and
their legs greatly modified in shape. Darwin
has explained Sexual Diomorphism by his
theory of Sexual Selection. Sexual Diomorphism reaches its acme in the males of certain
solitary barnacles; they are minute, very much
reduced in structure, living inside the mantle

cavity of the female, where they are anchored by their antennae."

The same authority explains the above reference to Sexual Selection as follows:

"The principle of Sexual Selection depends, as Darwin states, not on a struggle for existence, but on a struggle between the males for possession of the females. The result is not death to the unsuccessful competitor, but few or no offspring. In many cases, however, victory depends not on general vigor, but on the possession of special weapons confined to the male sex, as the spurs of the cock or the horns of the stag. The war is perhaps severest between the males of polygamous animals, and these seem oftenest provided with special weapons of offence. Among birds the contest is often less gross and fierce, the males rivalling each other in attracting the females by their powers of song or display of plumage.

"Darwin concludes that when the males and females of any animal have the same habits of life, but differ in structure, color, or ornament, such differences have been mainly caused by sexual selection; i.e., by individual males having had, in successive generations, some slight advantages over other males, in their weapons, means of defence, or charms, and having transmitted these advantages to their male offspring. Although Wallace does not accept the theory of Sexual Selection, claiming that bright colors were originally normal in both sexes, but have been eliminated in the females, yet the facts seem to substantiate the views of Darwin. As observed by Romanes, it is 'a theory wholly and completely distinct from Natural Selection'."

Whatever may have been the predominant evolutionary cause leading to this distinctive marking and equipment of the male animals, the fact remains unquestioned that the female animals are attracted by these special characteristics of the male, and bestow their favors upon the attractively marked individual males, the less fortunate males being comparatively discarded. Nature has evolved this means of attracting the sex-element of the females by the special physical appearance or weapons of the male; the manifestation of such characteristics is unquestionably a derivative sex attribute. The attractive male animal succeeds in propagating his kind, just as truly as the attractive flower tends toward greater fertility by reason of being favored by the visiting insects which serve the purpose of fertilization.

The **primary** characteristics or attributes of Sex are those immediately or very closely associated with the processes of fertilization, namely, (a) the power of producing respectively the sperm and the ova, and (b) the possession of the organs necessary for conjugation, oviposition, gestation, parturition and nutrition of the immature young in any stage. The secondary, or derivative characteristics of Sex are those which are concerned with "the differences between the sexes is size, shape, appearance, ornamentation, armament, color and coloration, voice, and instincts and habits not directly associated with the reproductive processes."

The primary or original sexual characteristics or attributes are those which are concerned directly with the sexual act of fertilization. The secondary or derivative sexual characteristics are those which are concerned with the attraction between the individuals of the two sexes, whereby at least some degree of "sexual selection" is performed—in the "love making" or "falling in love" of the animals, and in the simpler corresponding processes in plant-life.

Darwin devoted much attention to these secondary or derivative sexual characteristics in animals, and, as before stated, explained the same by his theory of Sexual Selection, i.e., the hypothesis that as the females almost invariably select as mates those individual males so attractively marked, these special characteristics thereafter in time become fixed in the male offspring—the unattractive males, having fewer offspring, being unable to exert a corresponding influence on the characteristics of the species.

These secondary or derivative sexual attributes or characteristics, however, are not universally present in the animal-world. On the contrary, among many mammals, and among many birds, there are no distinguishing marks between the two sexes excepting those of the primary sexual attributes or characteristics, i.e., the reproductive organism itself. But, almost invariably, when such secondary characteristics are found in a species, they are found in the male animal rather than in the female. In many cases the male possesses the attractive markings, etc., only during the mating season, thus showing clearly and unmistakably Nature's purpose in manifesting the distinction, and in her use of it.

Darwin's theory of Sexual Selection is well illustrated by the following quotation from one of his books: "Courage, pugnacity, perseverance, strength and size of body, weapons of all kinds, musical organs, both vocal and instrumental, bright colors, stripes and marks, and ornamental appendages, have all been indirectly gained by the one sex or the other, through the influence of love or jealousy, through the appreciation of the beautiful in sound, color or form, and through the exertion of a choice; and these powers of the mind manifestly depend upon the development of the cerebral system."

Another authority adds: "The secondary characters to be accounted for are confined to one sex, and are in close relation with the breeding season and the breeding habits. In those cases where they differ from the females, the males are the most active in courtship, and the best armed, and are rendered the most attractive in many ways. They fight with their rivals for the possession of the female, or display their attractions before her, and either by conquest, or being preferred, have an advantage of less favored males."

With this understanding of the nature, cause and reason of the many secondary characteristics appearing in the animal world, you will read a new and strange meaning in your experience of the world of living things. You will see the Presence of Sex in the living world around you, and will see the fine hand of Nature manipulating the appearance and actions of all living things in direct relation to the Power of Sex. Were the activities of Sex to be brought to a sudden termination, not only would the world of living things soon die out for want of fresh material, but even while it survived with constantly decreasing force and lessening numbers it would be a far different, and a far less attractive and less beautiful world than it now appears to be to our senses.

The above thought is brought out more

clearly in the following quotation from Grant Allen, the English naturalist, who says:

"Everything high and ennobling in our nature springs directly out of the sexual instinct. Its alliance is wholly with whatever is purest and most beautiful within us. To it we owe our brightest colors, graceful forms, melodious sounds, and rhythmical motion. To it we owe the evolution of music, of poetry, of romance, of belles lettres; the evolution of sculpture, of decorative art, of dramatic entertainment. To it we owe the entire existence of our esthetic sense, which is, in the last resort, a secondary sexual attribute. From it springs the love of beauty; around it, too, are grouped the paternal and marital relations; the love of little pattering feet and baby laughter; the home with all the associations that cluster around it; in one word, the heart and all that is best in it.

"If we look around among the inferior animals, we shall see that germs of everything which is best in humanity took their rise with them in the sexual instinct. The song of the nightingale, or of Shelley's skylark, is a song that has been acquired by the bird himself to charm the ears of his attentive partner. The ·chirp of the cricket, the cheerful note of the grasshopper, the twittering of the sparrow, the pleasant caw of the rookery—all these as Darwin showed, are direct products of sexual selection. Every pleasant sound that greets our

ears from the hedge or copse in a summer walk
has the self-same origin.

"If we were to take away from the country
the music conferred upon it by the sense of sex, ·
we should have taken away every vocal charm
it possesses, save the murmuring of brooks and
the whispering of breezes through the leaves.
No thrush, no blackbird, no linnet would be
left us; no rattle of the night-jar over the twi-
light fields; no chirp of insect, no chatter of
tree-frog, no cry of cuckoo from the leafy
covert. The whippoorwill and the bobolink
would be as mute as the serpent. Every beautiful voice in wild nature, from the mocking-
bird to the cicada, is, in essence, a love-call;
and without such love-calls the music of the
fields would be mute, the forests would be
silent."

Had Allen extended his thought to the realm
of the plants, he would have been able to have
emphasized quite as forcibly our dependence
upon the sexual energies and influence of the
world of plants, flowers, and fruits. For without Sex, there would be no beautiful buds and
flowers upon which to feast our eyes. The
rose, the lily, the violet, and all the great array
of wild and cultivated flowers would be absent
from our sight, and their fragrance would no
longer delight our sense of smell. · No longer
would the wealth of cherry-blossoms charm
us; no longer the perfume of the honey-suckle

or lilac, the heliotrope or the sweet-pea, refresh us. For these flowers are not only the sexual organism of the plant, but their beauty and fragrance arise by reason of Nature's clever plan to attract to them the insects needed to fertilize them, and thus to promote the process of reproduction of their kind.

Likewise, absent also would be the delicious fruits and berries—those cleverly designed carriers of the seed of the plants and trees; gone also would be the nuts, great and small. Missing, likewise, would be the seeds of the wheat, rye, barley, and corn—the grains which form such an important element of our food.

Were Sex to cease its entire manifestation in plant-life for even a single season, all animal-life would perish—and, before perishing, we would gaze sadly upon a world robbed of a great portion of its beauty, and of its appeals to sight, taste and smell. These things, so true and important to us, are too close to us to be appreciated; it is only when we consider the effects of their possible absence that we begin to realize the all-important part played by Sex in the world in which we live, and move and have our being, even apart from the part it plays in our own personal lives.

No less wonderful, no less powerful, is the effect produced by Sex upon the emotional nature of living things, upon the desires arising from them, and upon the actions resulting from such desires. Such an important place in our mental and emotional world, and in our world of will, does Sex occupy, that were she to withdraw or suspend her activities and influence there would be but comparatively little left for living creatures to feel, to desire, to will to do, and to manifest in action. Directly or indirectly Sex is involved in the greater portions of our feelings, desires and actions of will. Often hidden, Sex usually will be found to be present, exerting a potent though silent and subtle influence upon feeling, thought, desire, will and acts.

To begin with the lower forms of life in the animal kingdom, we find that even there is to be found the ever-present and ever-active influence of Sex in the feelings, desires and acts of the living creature. Not only is exhibited there the primary urge of Sex in the direction of matehood and the cooperation of the male and female in the fundamental reproductive processes, but there also are found the derivative manifestations of feeling, desire, and action which are concerned with the protection of the female, the provision of shelter for the mother and the young where this is necessary, and the subsequent defence of the young together with the provision for their food and nourishment.

Even the fishes, the insects, and other lowly forms of life manifest the feeling, desire, and

will to protect their eggs, and their young offspring. Quite elaborate arrangements are made
by these creatures for the future welfare of
their offspring, the eggs being placed in close
proximity to the food supply, and where they
may not readily be destroyed by their natural
enemies. Some of the insects place their eggs
either upon, or in the bodies of other living
creatures; these bodies being the proper food
for the young insects when hatched from the
egg. One is amazed in reading scientific works
upon Insect Life, such as Fabre's for instance,
to discover how complex and ingenious are
some of the devices of the parent insect directed to this end.

Of course, you may say, this is "merely instinct," but instinct is but the more or less unconscious habit which has arisen from previous
deliberate and conscious action. Moreover,
even if it be but instinct, the manifestation of
that instinct is accompanied by feeling, desire
and will-action on the part of the creature. To
the insect, as well as to the bird, and as well
as to the higher animal, the eggs or the young
are objects of intense solicitude and interest.
Some insects will die in defence of their eggs;
.and the fact that birds will often sacrifice
themselves in the protection of their eggs or
their young is too well known to require argument. If you have ever tried to disturb a "setting" hen, you will realize the depth and in-

tensity of her affection for her precious eggs,
and her ardent desire to cover them and to
keep them warm—even though she be unconscious of the ultimate object of her endeavors.

In bird-life is to be seen the performance of
arduous labors in the building of the nest, and
in its subsequent protection from natural enemies. The elemental selfishness of the adult
birds is overcome by their deep feeling and desire to feed the young when hatched, or, in
some cases, to feed the brooding mother-bird.
In certain species, the male bird alternates
with the female in the "setting" process. Some
male fishes watch over and protect the egg-
nest or place of deposit and shelter. All of
these and similar actions are performed simply
because the creature "wants to"—because its
feelings and desires prompt such action. For
the time being, the instinct of self-preservation
is secondary to that of the protection of the offspring—a clear manifestation of Sex influence.

The mutual attraction, desire for companionship, and "love" of living creatures for their
mates (apart from the attraction of the direct
sexual act) undoubtedly arises from the deep-
rooted instinct or desire for the protection of
the young. This is evidenced by the fact that
where the protection of the father-animal is
not necessary, then there is no sign of "love"
between the parents; and that where such need
is the greatest, there is the "love" between the

parents greatest in power and in length of duration. The measure of the "love" of the mated animals, and of the duration thereof, is directly proportioned to the need of the protection of the young by the parents, particularly by the male parent.

The eggs of the spider require no parental care: hence the male and female spiders "love" only during the moment of actual intercourse —the female frequently devours her mate immediately afterward. The eggs of the bee require no parental care, the neuters attending to this; hence the male drones are put to death after their services have been rendered, and the mother-bee, the queen, evinces no interest whatever in her offspring, or in her mates after the act of fertilization is performed.

In the case of certain insects, the living substance of the male parent is actually drawn from his body and into the body of the female, naught but the dead shell of the devoted male mate being left; the females of certain species of spiders devour their mates after fertilization is effected; the food thus obtained by eating or absorption is employed for the building of the egg-substance in the body of the female. Nature is very "matter of fact" in the love-making of these creatures; there is very little sentiment wasted in the matter, and the flame of passion burns but for a moment, then dies out forever.

Snakes and other reptiles which deposit their eggs in a safe place and then leave them, or which bring forth their young fully equipped for life work, usually manifest no affection between the mates following the sexual act; and such creatures seem devoid of paternal affection: Nature evidently does not provide such emotions where they serve no good purpose or need in the reproductive offices and the subsequent protection of the offspring. Most birds, while ardent lovers and devoted mates during the mating and brooding season, and while usually willing to sacrifice themselves for the mate or for their young during that period, lose the mutual affection after the need of that period is passed—though in a few exceptional cases the affection continues over longer periods—sometimes even for life, it is claimed.

The cuckoos and similar birds which deposit their eggs in the nests of other birds, there to be hatched along with the legitimate brood of the foster parents, are inveterate polygamists and polyandrists, cohabiting indiscriminately and showing not the slightest signs of permanent or continued affection for their whilom mates. On the other hand, those birds and other animals whose young require careful and continued attention always are found to manifest a strong "mate-love" during the period of that need. Nature has evidently established this rule for the protection of the young, and the continuance of the species.

Darwin explains this upon the theory that the ancestral creatures who manifested the necessary "mate-love" transmitted it to their numerous well-protected offspring; while those not manifesting it had but comparatively few offspring to inherit their unfavorable tendencies: consequently, the habit and custom soon became set and fixed in the species. Other thinkers, however, while admitting that the rule would work out as Darwin indicated, nevertheless believe that the original impulse was there in the beginning, and that in addition to the "survival value" of such habits there is also to be taken into consideration an "unconscious intuition" which manifests in action through instinct, and which gradually becomes set and fixed as habit.

In the higher animals, or of such species of them in which the young creatures require the protection and food-supplying offices of the male parent, there is often seen a marked and often long-continued attachment between the parent animals, and a comparatively permanent companionship even after the mating and ·breeding season. Among the higher wild animals, mating is often comparatively permanent, sometimes enduring for the life of the two mates; and here, as might be expected, there is to be found a need for such association, for

by the time one brood is ready to be cast off
to pursue life on their own account, Nature
has begun preparations for the following brood.
This rule is true among the lower races of
man, as well, and in about the same degree.

The human infant is probably the most help-
less thing in the world—it can do nothing for
itself except to nurse its mother's breast, and
it must even be held up during that performance. Moreover, its period of dependence continues for a long time, so long in fact that its
younger brother or sister is held in Nature's
vision before the first child is ready to do anything much for itself. As might be expected,
here we find a comparatively strong and long-
continued attachment between the parents,
even in primitive human society. Here, again,
according to Darwin, the "survival value" of
such a custom is great, and soon becomes set
and fixed as a habit of the race.

As mankind advances in culture, knowledge,
and experience, there occurs the grafting of
many new and strange mental and emotional
growths upon the parent stock of human love
for the mate. The original purpose, need and
instinct is always there—Nature attends carefully to this—but there exists in addition many
new requirements of the emotional nature
which often cause the original and elemental
urge to be overlooked, at least for a time.

As Carpenter says: "Nature (personifying

under this term the more unconscious, even
though human, instincts and forces) takes
pretty good care in her own way that Sex
shall not be neglected. She has her own purposes to work out, which in a sense have nothing to do with the individual—her racial purposes. But she acts in the rough, with tremendous sweep and power, and with little adjustment to or consideration for the later developed and more conscious and intelligent ideals
of humanity."

Nordau says: "The more highly cultivated,
the more original, the more differentiated an
individual, the more complex the qualities
which he attributes to the longed-for and expected individual of the opposite sex. . . . .
The lower and simpler the ideal, the easier it is
for the individual to find the realization of it
in corporate form. Hence, common and simple
natures fall in love very easily, and find no
difficulty in replacing the object of their love
by another; while delicate and complex natures
find it a long and tedious task to discover their
ideal or anything approximating it, in real
life, and in giving it a successor if it happens
to lose it."

Human love between the sexes may be of
high or of low degree; of extreme elemental
simplicity of character, or of extreme complex-
ity of nature; it may manifest itself in many
ways—sometimes the physical manifestation

being almost lost sight of for the time being, owing to the power and force of the other elements and factors involved. But, high or low, simple or complex (even in the form of the most ideal Platonic Friendship) the element of Sex is always there, and sometimes that element manifests its force with a terrifying sudden directness and intensity when and where the least expected. In the Unconscious of each individual, Sex abides in all its power, awaiting its time and opportunity to manifest itself—those who are wise never lose sight of this fact: the unwise ignore or deny it, and this folly in many cases results in their undoing.

Were Nature, in her phase and form of Sex, to cease her activities, and to withdraw her influence over the feelings, desires, will and actions of mankind, then all of Man's feelings, desires, will and actions which result directly or indirectly from Sex Attraction would cease. Such a change occurring overnight would cause an entirely different world to present itself in experience with the dawn of the new day. Seventy-five per cent, or more, of human action then would have ceased to manifest itself. All the consciousness of differentation between the sexes then having ceased, all the attractions between the sexes would have come to an end; and all sexual feelings, desires and tendencies toward action, all will and all voluntary action resulting from such feelings and desires would cease to be experienced or manifested by men and women. All would then be practically of one sex, or rather, sexless, in feeling, emotion, will, habits and actions! This indeed would be a new world—a world almost inconceivable to our imagination.

In such a world, everything which now causes a man's feelings concerning a woman to be different from his feelings concerning a man, or vice-versa; everthing which now causes a man to act differently toward a woman than toward a man, and vice-versa;—all these things would have vanished, and would be remembered but as a dream. A moment's consideration will cause you to realize what tremendous changes this would cause in our world of experience. Everything would be topsy-turvy, inside-out, "at sixes and sevens." Add to this the loss of the element of love of offspring, the desire to protect offspring, all family life and action, and you would have Chaos. Social life, business life, industrial life, art, music, and all else, would be changed beyond recognition, if not indeed be entirely destroyed.

Combine into a single, compositive imaginative picture the idea of the withdrawal of Sex from the world of plant-life, the world of animal-life, and the world of human-life, and you will begin to realize at least faintly the all-important part played by Sex in the processes of Nature, and the tremendous force and power exerted therein by Sex, as well as the almost infinite extension of the influence of Sex throughout all Nature and her manifestations. Sex, symbollized as Love, not only brings the world of living things into being, but it also keeps that world alive and in action. Well did the old song inform us that "It's Love that makes the world go 'round."

IV

TRANSMUTATION OF SEX-ENERGY

In the preceding section of this book we have considered the more commonly and better known secondary or derivative attributes and characteristics of Sex. Therein, you have perceived that Sex-Energy is directed by Nature not alone along the channels of the primary activities of Sex concerned directly with the performance of the sexual functions and with the processes of the physical generation and development of the offspring, but also along certain special channels which are concerned with the evolution and maintenance of certain special physical, mental, and emotional characteristics of the living forms—which special characteristics would not have been developed, and would not be maintained, were the Sex-Energy inoperative.

In the present section you are asked to consider an additional, and very important, derivative manifestation of Sex-Energy—one in which the general physical, mental, and emotional nature of the individual (apart from its employment in purely sexual activities) is strengthened, invigorated and given power by the indirect activities of Sex-Energy. In short, you will be shown that Sex-Energy may be, and indeed is; employed by Nature in the processes of Regeneration of the individual as well as in those of Generation or Reproduction.

This phase of the operation of Sex-Energy is not so well known as are its other phases, and, indeed, for a long time Science was disposed to ignore or to deny the existence of such phase, leaving the knowledge of it, and the discussion concerning it, to the non-scientific layman. But certain recent discoveries of Science have awakened new interest in the subject on the part of scientific observers. Science now having been supplied with a valid physiological basis for thought along these lines, it is extremely probable that the next twenty years will bring important scientific investigations and discoveries concerning the operation and the application of the natural laws involved in this particular subject.

As we have previously informed you, the esoteric philosophers and arcane schools of the ancient world recognized the presence and the operation of these natural laws of Regeneration, and made the study of them an important branch of their work and teaching. But here, as in other branches of knowledge, these ancient thinkers did not direct their thought along what are now known as "scientific lines." Instead, they were in the habit of explaining all known facts by reference to occult causes—

often supernatural causes. They were right concerning their facts, but their inductive reasoning was weakened by their habit of taking it for granted that "causes" were to be found only in the realms of the supernatural and not in Nature herself. The modern scientific mind, on the contrary, seeks ever to find a natural cause for all effects and activities perceived to exist in the natural world.

Accordingly, these ancient thinkers usually attributed both Generation and Regeneration to "occult" forces, or supernatural powers. They regarded Sex-Energy as a Divine Principle in many cases, or else as a reflection of the Secret Creative Energy which they held to exist apart from the world though acting upon it. Modern Science, on the contrary, regards the Sex-Energy merely as a phase of the manifestation of "That Infinite and Eternal Energy from which all things proceed," and which is found present and operative in all natural processes. Modern Science finds in Nature all that the ancients were accustomed to regard as "super-natural," i.e., over and above Nature. It holds that "whatever is, is natural"—that whatever is possible of human knowledge, or ·in human experience, is "natural," and that even where causes are as yet unknown they must be assumed to be in Nature and not outside of it.

The ancients knew little or nothing about the actual physiological processes of Generation as these are known to modern Science. They regarded Generation and Reproduction as caused by the union and mingling of two occult "forces" which abode in the beings of male and female creatures. Modern Science, in its branch known as Physiology, on the contrary, knows that Generation or Reproduction is caused by the union of the reproductive cells of the parent creatures—the "sperm" cells and the cells of the "ova" or egg. The miscroscope has revealed the character and the appearance of the spermatozoa and the ova, and the physical and physiological processes of Reproduction and Generation are definitely known and taught. Life itself, it is true, lies beyond the microscope or the dissecting-knife—but Science at least is able to tell "just how Life works" in these processes.

In the same way, the ancients believed that Regeneration or the Transmutation of Sex-Energy was caused by a direction of the occult "forces" of Generation along new channels. Modern Science, however, whenever it has investigated the subject at all, has held that this Regeneration or Transmutation of Sex-Energy proceeds along the strict lines of physiological process. It holds that the sex-glands of the male and female secrete certain elements which make for the invigoration of the mental and physical nature of the man or woman, just as do certain other glands of the body secrete certain elements which produce decided and marked effects upon the mind and body of the individual in whose body they exist and are active. Such special secretion of the sex-glands being admitted or assumed as possible, Science finds no difficulty whatsoever in explaining the effects of Regeneration or Transmutation of Sex-Energy.

Even before the recent scientific discoveries of the effects resulting from the transplanation of the sex-glands into the bodies of the lower animals (and in a few instances into the bodies of human beings), there have been modern thinkers and writers upon the subject who have held that the sex-glands are capable of such secretion of a "regenerative element," and that in every individual the processes of Regeneration are operative to at least some extent; and that by the proper methods of application the secretion of these regenerative elements will be increased, and may be deliberately directed to the mental and physical processes of the individual. Such a conception is usually found to lie at the base of the teaching of certain modern schools of thought which advocate chastity, continence and sexual temperance on the part of their followers.

Thus, you see, these modern thinkers are really marching abreast with the ancient think-

ers along the same lines—so far as the facts of
the case are concerned. Though the ancients
explained these facts by the theory of "occult
forces," or supernatural powers operative in·
the natural world, while the modern thinkers
explain the same facts by the accepted laws of
physiological process, there is a common
agreement upon the facts of the case so far as
the effects and phenomena are concerned. The
effects are agreed upon as true, valid and existing, in both cases—though the "causes" assumed to account for the effects are quite different, at least on the surface of thought.

The following quotations from writers on
this subject during the past twenty-five years,
or thereabouts, will serve to illustrate how the
current of modern thought has been running
in this direction—even before the recent discoveries concerning the internal secretions of
the other glands of the body, and of the transplanation of the sex-glands, to both of which
we have just referred. In each of the following quotations the writer is either a recognized
medical authority upon the subject, or else a
layman who has given careful attention to,
made careful observations, and conducted careful experiments along these lines. There are
many others of equal authority who might
have also been quoted in this connection—the
following are merely a few selected from the

great number of intelligent and competent authorities available.

Dr. Kellogg, advocating the continent life, says: "The sexual function is double in its purpose. First, the sexual organs are always active, even when not excited to such a degree as to obtrude their activity upon the consciousness, as they supply the body with a needed vital stimulus and regulator. Secondly, they furnish the only means by which the physical life of the individual and the perpetuation of the race may be accomplished. In neither of these important functions is the personal gratification of the individual the primary consideration. The exercise of the sexual function with a purely selfish purpose would seem to be a debasement of the sacred function in which man approaches most nearly to the creative power of which he is the image."

Dr. Nicholas says: "It is a medical and physiological fact that the best blood of the body goes to form the elements of reproduction in both sexes. In a pure and orderly life this matter is reabsorbed. It goes back into the circulation ready to form the finest brain, nerve and muscular tissue. This life of man, carried back and diffused through his system, makes him manly, strong, brave, heroic. The suspension of the use of the generative organs is attended with a notable increase of bodily and mental vigor and spiritual life. Nature finds another use for the unexpended sexual energy in employing it for the building up of a keener brain, and more vital and enduring nerves and muscles."

Dr. Kellogg, says again: "Recent investigations have shown that the sexual glands are useful, not only as a means of race-perpetuation, but for the physical well-being of the individual, through the vital stimulus exercised by them through the influence of their peculiar secretion upon the processes of development and nutrition. In view of this fact, it is evident that, so far as the individual is concerned, physical benefit is to be looked for, not in the loss of the secretion of the sexual glands, but in its retention and appropriation. In other words, reproduction is accomplished at the sacrifice of individual interests, a law which prevails throughout the whole organic world, being, in some instances, so pronounced that the development of progeny is accomplished only through the death of one or more parents. These discoveries afford thoroughly satisfactory and scientific explanations of two facts which heretofore have rested solely upon a basis of observation and experience, viz.: (1) That continence is favorable to physical vigor; (2) that sexual intemperance is productive of exhaustion and debility to a most extraordinary degree."

Professor Acton says: "Physiologically considered, it is not a fact that the power of secretion is annihilated in well-formed adults leading a healthy life, and yet remaining continent. No continent man need be deterred by the apocryphal fear of atrophy from leading a chaste life. It is a device of the unchaste, a lame excuse for their own incontinence, unfounded on any physiological law. I may state that, after many years' experience, I have never seen an instance of atrophy of the generative organs from this cause. I have, it is true, met the complaint; but in what classes of cases does it occur? It arises, in all instances, from the exactly opposite cause, abuse!"

Professor Newton says: "It is important to know that there are other uses for the procreative element than the generation of physical offspring, and far better uses than its waste in momentary pleasure. It may, indeed, be better wasted than employed in imposing unwelcome burdens upon toiling and outraged women. But there should be no waste. This element when retained in the system may be coined into new thoughts, perhaps new inventions, grand conceptions of the true, the beautiful, the useful; or into fresh emotions of joy, and impulses of kindness and blessing to all around. This is, in fact, but another department of procreation. It is the procreation of thoughts, ideas, feelings of good-will, intu-

itions of truth—that is, it is the procreation on
the mental and spiritual planes, instead of on
the physical plane. It is really just as really a
part of the generative function as is the begetting of physical offspring. It is by far the
greater part, for physical procreation can
ordinarily be participated in but seldom, while
mental and spiritual procreation may and
should go on through all our earthly lives—
yea, through all our immortal existence."

Dr. Stockham says: "Physicists have demonstrated with incontrovertible facts that it is
eminently healthy to conserve the vital principle. The seminal secretion has a wonderfully immanent value; and, if retained, is absorbed into the system and adds enormously
to man's magnetic, mental, and spiritual force.
In ordinary married life this force is constantly being wasted. Other things being equal, the
man who wisely conserves is improved in concentrated mental and physical power and ef-
fectiveness, like a Daniel amid his companions.
He builds, and constructs, he is the organizer
and executive head of industries, he is the
orator and the inventor. He is the leader of
great movements, because his power is drawn
from an inexhaustible storage battery. Although woman has not the sperm to conserve,
yet equally with man she has the thrilling
potency of sex, that, when well directed, heals

sensitive nerves, vitalizes the blood, and re-
stores tissue."

Dr. Talmey says: "Continence, if long continued, has been claimed to be the cause of im-
potence. But there is no valid reason for this
belief. To prove the harmfulness of continence, an analogue is brought forward between
the atrophy of a muscle in enforced idleness
and the injury to the sex organs in enforced
abstinence. But the proof is somewhat feeble.
The essential organs of generation are not
muscles, but glands; and who has ever heard
of a tear gland atrophying for want of crying.
* * * The instinct of generation has been compared with the instinct of hunger and thirst,
and as the latter must be satisfied, so it is held
the former must be gratified. But there is no
proper parallelism between these two instincts.
Food and drink are vital necessities of the
organism from the first day of conception, to
replace the stuffs consumed in the metabolism
of the vital functions. The generative instinct
appears a number of years after birth, hence
does not serve any vital necessity."

Dr. Stockham says: "The testes may be considered analogous to the salivary and lachrymal glands, in which there is no fluid secreted
except at the demand of their respective functions. The thought of food makes the mouth
water for a short time only, while the presence
of food causes abundant yield of saliva. It is

customary for physiologists to assume that the
spermatic secretion is analogous to bile, which,
when once formed, must be expelled. But substitute the word 'tears' for bile, and you put
before the mind an idea entirely different.
Tears, as falling drops, are not essential to life
and health. A man may be in perfect health
and not cry once in five or fifty years. The
lachrymal fluid is ever present, but in such
small quantities that it is unnoticed. Where
are the tears while they remain unshed? They
are ever ready, waiting to spring forth when
there is an adequate cause, but they do not
accumulate and distress the man because they
are not shed daily, weekly or monthly.

"The component elements of the tears are
prepared in the system, they are on hand, passing through the circulation, ready to mix and
flow whenever they are needed; but if they
mix, accumulate, and flow without adequate
cause, there is a disease of the lachrymal
glands. While there are no exact analogies in
the body, yet the tears and the spermatic
fluids are much more closely analogous in their
normal manner of secretion and use than are
the bile and the semen. Neither flow of tears
nor of semen is essential to life or health. Both
are largely under the control of the imagination, the emotions, the will; and the flow of
either is liable to be arrested in a moment of
sudden mental action. * * *

"The mammary gland is an apt illustration of the law of supply and demand. In its anatomical construction and physiological function is it not analogous to the seed-producing gland of the male? No one has ever hinted that it is essential for health that the natural lacteal fluid of the mammary gland must be continually or frequently secreted or expelled. It is not considered 'a physical necessity' or a demand of nature. Indeed, the contrary opinion prevails—that a too abundant flow of milk is derogative to healthful conditions. Milk flows in answer to the demand of a new-born infant, and, should it come at any other time than when thus demanded, it is considered a perversion of nature and an unnecessary drain upon the system. May it not prove that the unnecessary secretion and expulsion of the semen is as great a perversion of nature? May it not also prove that erectile tissue in action is not a positive evidence of secretion in the gland?"

Parkhurst, writing along the same general lines, says: "The prostatic fluid, according to Robin, is secreted at the moment of ejaculation. The remaining element of the spermatic secretion is produced, under normal circumstances, only as required, either for impregnation or for the maintenance of the affectional function. The theory that the sperm is naturally secreted only as it is required, brings it into harmony with other secretions. The tears, the saliva, and the perspiration, are always required in small quantities, and the secretion is continuous; but if required in large quantities, the secretion becomes great almost instantly. The mother's milk is chiefly secreted just as it is required for the infant, and when not required the secretion entirely ceases; yet it recommences the moment the birth of another child makes it necessary. * * *

"A man accustomed to abstinence will not suffer from any accumulation of secretions, while a man whose absorbing glands have never had trouble to take up the secretions, will be in trouble; just as a dairy cow which has not been milked will be in trouble, though if running wild she would never have any necessity for milking. . . . . . The objection that man needs physical relief from a continuous secretion, is answered by the admitted fact that men, not deficient in sexual vigor, live for months, and probably for years, in strict abstinence, without the physical inconvenience such as is often complained of by men who happen to be deprived of their accustomed indulgence for a week or two at a time."

An anonymous writer on the subject of "Sex Polarity" (the identity of whom, however, is known to the present writers), several years ago, said:

"Nature devotes a great amount of energy to the task of reproducing living forms. Many of the lower forms of life seem to live merely for the purpose of reproducing life—of passing along the flame of life from torch to torch. Nature's reproductive energies are highly concentrated, and are wonderfully potent. The amount of creative energy concentrated and compressed into the mustard seed is equal to that diffused over a whole large plant—in fact, the essence of the entire creative energy which is to serve the plant for its lifetime must be stored up within the seed itself, for the vital force cannot come from outside, although the outer nourishment is needed to build up the physical shape, form and substance of the plant. The germ of the animal contains within itself enough stored-up energy to carry the creature through its normal period of life. In the processes of reproduction and procreation, Nature avails herself of her inner powers, and every minute she works miracles of concentration and conservation of energy.

"The ancient occultists recognized the wonderful power stored in the reproductive organism, which is given out not only in the act of 'actual reproduction and procreation, but which may also be dissipated in the unnatural excesses and practices to which the race is addicted. They soon discovered that this wonderful concentrated power could be used not only for the purpose of generation, but also for the purpose of re-generation of the life activities within one's own body, the exhaustion of which occurs if the vital forces be given out in procreation or waste. In other words, that the wonderfully concentrated forces of the sexual functions, if not otherwise used or dissipated, might be used by the individual himself or herself in re-energizing, re-charging, or re-generating the vital powers within his or her own organism. This was one of the reasons that continence was enjoined as a duty upon the members of the ancient esoteric and occult brotherhoods and sisterhoods. * * *

"Outside of the list of the occult brotherhoods, all of whose staunch members were strictly continent, history gives us a long list of eminent men who followed the practice of continence, which indicates the correctness of the old occult teachings of generation. Newton, Kant, Paschal, Michael Angelo, Plato, and many other eminent men were strictly continent. All the great occultists and mystics of ancient times observed strict continence. The Greek athletes training for the great Olympic games were required to observe strict continence, the experience of the trainers being that by following this course the athletes were able to conserve their strength and vigor much better than otherwise. The prize-fighters of today are compelled by their trainers and back-ers to observe strict continence during the period of training for the combat. Many of the former 'champions' who 'went to pieces' suddenly, owe their downfall to a violation of this rule."

Dr. Henderson, reporting his experience among men subjected to great strain in tropical countries, said: "I have seen many suffer severely, destroying their strength, health, and happiness, and life, by following the promptings of their unbridled passions. Need I say that I have never seen a man suffer from keeping himself pure." Dr. Talmey says: "The conventional view that incontinence in men is a necessary condition of health must be corrected. Instead of the popular fallacy that a young man is physically the worse for a clean moral life, the entire weight of the world's foremost medical scholars is unreservedly of the opinion that he is physically better for it. It is recognized by the highest authorities that continence is perfectly compatible with the most perfect health. Chastity, properly understood, is health; it never does harm to mind or body. It is the consensus of the opinions of the great medical thinkers that it is not 'prejudicial to the health of man to keep his body clean."

Dr. Armitage says: "A writer has said: 'Chastity, yes, even continence, is the prime necessity of the successful athlete.' It is further urged in support of this view, that the male animals, even those so active sexually as the bull, are known to maintain perfect health and vigor when forced to live apart from the' females. Moreover, the best breeders of animals know very well that restraint and moderation on the part of their male animals will result in an improvement of the stock, as compared with the opposite course." Dr. Kellogg also has reminded us that: "Breeders of stock who wish to secure sound progeny will not allow the most robust stallion to associate with mares as many times during the whole season as some of these salacious human males perform a similar act within a month."

Dr. Sperry says: "It is true that moderate sexual activity tends, temporarily, at least, to increase and intensify the sexual impulses and energies; but such exaltation of sexuality is not evidence of increased general healthfulness and efficiency. If the usual physiological expression of sexuality be held in check, its energies (which most easily, it is true, seek expression in sexual lines) are transferred to the other departments, to which they contribute largely in the life and power of each, and in the material addition of general vigor. The force then becomes creative, or productive, in other lines. In other words, sexuality, if it be denied the reproductive expression, and provided that it also be kept from artificial excitation, seems to develop a sort of dynamic force or energy, which the nutritive, the motor, and the relational departments can use to their individual and collective advantage.

"On the other hand, those who unnaturally or excessively expend along sexual lines what may seem to them to be exclusively sexual energy, available only for sexual expression, thereby deprive the system at large of what might have become general stimulation and vitality. Indeed, the sexual department of a continent adult seems to be a sort of storage battery of vitality, a veritable reservoir for surplus energy. This energy, which seems so like a tremendous dynamic force, may be expended just as each individual shall elect: it may be wasted in lustful and abnormal sensuality; or it may be used partly for the legitimate purposes of reproduction, and the remainder in lustful practices; or it may be expended in exalting and intensifying the nutritive, the muscular, and the mental life. This remarkable fact is of great practical importance."

Illustrations and quotations along the same lines might be continued at much greater length, but those which have just been presented will serve to give you a general idea of the thought concerning this subject which has been current among thinking persons for the last twenty-five years and more. Some of these modern thinkers are fully cognizant of the resemblance of their thought to that of the ancients whose minds had been directed along the same channels; others seem not to have been aware of the fact that as long ago as twenty-five hundred years or more the thoughts of men were striving to uncover the workings of this same principle.

You will note, however, that these modern seekers after truth along these lines employ the terms of physiology instead of those of metaphysics or of occultism. They have been striving to account for the phenomena of Regeneration or Transmutation of Sex-Energy by the theories of "gland secretions" and similar physiological processes. This is especially remarkable in view of the fact that, at the time when most of the above-quoted statements of fact and theory were written by the persons named, the recent scientific discoveries concerning the effect of the secretions of the ductless glands had not as yet been made, nor had there been as yet conducted the recent experiments in gland transplantation which have given positive evidence of the proof of the general theory of Regeneration or Transmutation of Sex-Energy.

V

THE DUCTLESS GLANDS

Advanced investigators in the ranks of physiological research have in recent years made very important discoveries concerning the secretions of the various glands of the animal body (including of course the human body), and their effect upon the health, vigor, growth and general functioning of the entire body. The "ductless glands" of the body, especially, have been found to secrete substances of the greatest value in the physiological processes, the absence of which has been found to cause deterioration and degeneracy of parts of the body, and the stimulation of which by artificial methods has been found to cause renewed activity, strength and vigor to such parts.

The term "Secretion," in the sense in which the term is employed in physiology, means: "Any substance secreted, i. e., separated from the blood and elaborated into a new substance." The term "Gland," as employed in physiology, means: "An organ whose function is that of secreting some substance to be used in, or to be eliminated from, the body."

Physiology divides the glands into two general classes, viz,. (1) the true secreting glands,

and (2) the ductless glands. The true secreting glands are defined as: "The special organs
which are intended for the production of the
chief secretions; as e.g., the Lachrymal Glands,
the Mammary Glands, the Salivary Glands, the
Liver, the Pancreas, and the Kidneys." The
principal ductless glands, according to the customary classification, are as follows: the Suprarenal Capsules, the Spleen, the Thymus,
the Thyroid, the Parathyroids, the Pituitary
Body, and the Pineal Glands; and, although
orthodox physiology vigorously resents and
combats the suggestion, the advanced investigators hold that the Testes and the Ovaries
are additional ductless glands, and that they
secrete subtle substances as do the other ductless glands, in addition to serving the better
known office of cell-formation for reproductive
purposes.

In the present inquiry we have little or no
concern with the so-called true secreting
glands, viz., the glands secreting the saliva,
the tears, the sweat, the bile, the pancreatic
juices, the milk, etc. These glands and their
secretions, highly important though they are,
are different in structure and in office from the
other great class of glands which we are called
upon to consider in our investigations concerning the processes of Regeneration. Accordingly, we shall now pass them by with the
above scant mention.

The Ductless Glands. The following definition of the Ductless Glands, taken from an authoritative reference work, represents the orthodox view of their character and function:

"Glands of the second class, i. e., the Ductless Glands, resemble those of the first class, i. e., the True Secreting Glands, in external conformation and in the possession of a solid parenchymatous tissue, but differ from them in the absence of a duct or opening for the removal of the products of secretion; and, indeed, except in the case of the Thymus, no material resembling a secreted product is yielded by any of them. In all of them the tissue mainly consists of cells and nuclei, with a great abundance of blood vessels. They furnish necessary material to the body in some as yet uncertained way. If they are removed by operation, or are absent from birth, or atrophied during life, the result is a condition of disease. * * * The Ductless Glands seem to produce some substance of great importance to the well-being of the body; but what it is, and how it affects the organism, are still involved in difficulties. However, as they are all closely associated with the blood system, they may as well be called vascular glands."

The reluctance of orthodox physiologists to admit the Ductless Glands, and especially the Testes and the Ovaries, to the category of true secreting glands, which is evident in the above quotation, is still more evident in the following additional quotation from the same authoritative orthodox reference work:

"Neither a definition nor a classification of glands has yet been agreed upon by comparative anatomists. Since the word itself offers no clew to its real meaning, we must attempt to define it from universally accepted examples. Among these may be mentioned salivary glands, lachrymal glands, sweat glands, and poison glands. All of these are organs which produce some particular substance from the blood with which they are supplied; furthermore this substance is not cellular nor living, but is a mere chemical product. These facts give us a clew to our definition, and we may say that a gland is any cell or group of cells **whose function is the production of a chemical substance,** usually fluid, peculiar to itself. Such a definition will not include all those organs to which the name 'gland' is given, but it will include all to which it ought to be applied. As an example of the incorrect use of the term, we may refer to 'reproductive' or 'genital' glands, as applied to the Testis or Ovary. These organs are not in any true sense glands, for they do not produce any chemical substance peculiar to themselves, but are simply the portions of the body where those cells are formed from which the next generation arises. So also the use of 'gland' in connection with the Suprarenal Capsule, the Pituitary Body, and the Pineal Body is incorrect and confusing."

The above statement that the term "gland" is properly to be limited so as not to include "all those organs to which the name 'gland' is given, but all to which it ought to be applied," is rather naive and ingenuous coming from such a source. In spite of this ultra-conservative position, however, advanced physiologists continue to apply the term "gland" to a constantly widening class of physical organs, the inclusion of the "genitals" being particularly insisted upon for good and valid reasons. Indeed, in other parts of the same reference book from which the above is quoted, we find the following statement: "The larger glands, such as the liver, kidney, pancreas, spleen, thyroid, thymus, testicle, and even the pituitary gland, have all their special diseases." So we feel justified in continuing to use the term "gland" as it actually is employed by advanced physiologists, instead of "as it ought to be" according to this ultra-orthodox authority.

Let us now consider in a little further detail the various Ductless Glands which, as we have seen, "furnish necessary material to the body in some as yet unascertained way, and which if they are removed by operation, or are absent from birth, or atrophied during life, result in a condition of disease"; and which "seem to produce some substance of great importance to the well-being of the body, though what it is and how it affects the organism, are still involved in difficulties."

The Thyroid Gland is a very vascular (i.e., vessel-containing) gland, lying on the front and sides of the larynx (i.e., upper end of the windpipe). It secretes and stores large amounts of iodine combinations and other chemical substances. The Thyroid secretions have trophic (i.e., nutritive) functions connected with the feeding or nourishing of the nervous system. Absence of the Thyroid Gland in children is characteristic of cretinism (i.e, idiocy accompanied by physical degeneracy and deformity, usually with goitre). Atrophy of the Thyroid Gland in adults causes myxoedema. Hypertrophy of the Thyroid Gland causes Basedow's disease. Removal of the Thyroid Gland is followed by diminished albumen and fat metabolism and lessened assimilation of sugar.

The function of the Thyroid Gland is stated to be that of "the production of an internal secretion which influences bodily nutrition in many ways." The prepared extract of the Thyroid Glands of sheep are employed in the treatment of diseases brought about by the atrophy or loss of functioning of the Thyroid Gland. This treatment consists of feeding the patient with the extract of the Thyroid Gland of sheep, or of the dried gland itself, together with phosphoric acid and iron tonics. Grafting of the Thyroid Gland, by transplanting the Thyroid of an animal upon the human patient, has also been employed. The prepared extract of the Thyroid Gland of the sheep, however, is the customary and generally preferred treatment.

The secretions of the Thyroid Gland stimulate and are stimulated by the secretions of the reproductive glands. A reference work says: "The Thyroid Gland has a very profound influence on nutrition, and disorders of it set up very definite physiological disturbances. Many nervous manifestations are due to a lack of its secretion, and accordingly these diseases are effectively treated by doses of Thyroid extract. The gland is also given in obesity, certain forms of neurasthenia, chronic rheumatism, chronic skin diseases, and disturbances of nutrition in the scalp, hair, and nails, and in many other conditions due to faulty metabolism. Thyroid must be given with care and in small doses at first, since it contains great possibilities for harm."

The Parathyroid Glands are small glands, closely connected with the Thyroid Gland though having quite different functions and offices. The Parathyroids are regarded as "a neuro-muscular balance wheel or control." Moreover, their secretions have antitoxic properties, and when these glands are removed tetanus, or lockjaw, frequently results. Unlike the Thyroid Gland, the secretions of the Parathyroids contain no iodine. They influence calcium metabolism, and the tetanus which results from their removal is believed to be caused by the withdrawal of calcium from the cells, as these conditions are promptly relieved by calcium feeding. The extract of the Parathryoids is employed in medical practice in paralysis agitans, tetanus, epilepsy and chorea.

The Pituitary Body, or Hypophysis, is a small glandular body situated at the base of the brain. It is described as "consisting of two portions, seeming to have different functions not as yet determined." In some manner its secretions seem to preside over the nutrition of the skeleton, and one of its portions is believed to stimulate the smooth muscle of the uterus. Its secretions are now employed in medical practice in connection with the unstriped muscle fibre of the uterus. Pituitary extract is administered to hasten labor, to stimulate the peristaltic action of the intestine in paretic conditions, in shock, in uterine hemorrhage, in amenorrhea, in polyuria, and also to stimulate the secretion of milk.

The Pineal Gland, or Epiphysis, is a small gland closely related to the Pituitary Body or Hypophysis, and situated just behind it. Its functions and offices are still somewhat in doubt, but leading authorities have held that during early life it influences the development of the reproductive organism; that it influences the deposit of subcutaneous fat; and that it has an effect upon general physical and mental growth and development. Advanced practitioners have treated cases of mentally backward children by administering a watery extract of the Pineal Gland of bullocks, and have reported favorable results.

The Thymus Gland is located in the neck of infants, behind the sternum or breastbone; it normally disappears in adult life, its functions being actively manifested in foetal life and early childhood. It is supposed to regulate nutrition and to control blood-pressure. It is intimately related to growth and development during its period of activity. It seems to be concerned with the retention of the calcium salts by the body and in the ossification of bone. In advanced medical practice an extract of the Thymus Gland is administered in the treatment of malnutrition, delayed development, rickets, certain forms of goitre, chlorosis, and rheumatoid arthritis.

The Adrenal Glands, or Suprarenal Capsules are two small bodies situated immediately in front of the upper end of each kidney. Their internal secretion is highly essential to life. Their function is to control the pigmentation of the skin, to arrest the action of poisons in the body, and to govern the vasomotor system regulating blood-pressure. Extracts of these secretions are employed in medical practice in eye, nose, and throat surgery, to control bleeding; and they are also administered internally in diseases marked by excessive bleeding or hemorrhages, also in some cases of tuberculosis and of asthma. The dried and prepared adrenal or suprarenal substances of animals constitute a powerful and valuable astringent and haemostatic. Suprarenal Extract and Adrenaline are recognized medicinal agents of great value; they relieve surgical shock, and in certain diseases prolong life for long periods.

The consideration of the above-stated subject of the Ductless Glands and their Internal Secretions results in the discovery of two important facts, viz., (1) that the Ductless Glands and their Internal Secretions play a most important part in the vital processes of the body; and (2) that these Internal Secretions of the Ductless Glands are so definitely designed for certain vital offices that extracts made from them have been, and are, effectively employed in the treatment of disease by advanced practitioners of medicine. Let us consider each of these two leading facts in a little further detail.

The Internal Secretions. The New International Encyclopaedia, in its article upon "Internal Secretions," says: "Internal Secretions are substances secreted by animal organs or tissues which preside over the development, growth, reproduction, and the chemical regulation of the body. They are also called Hormones, and are defined by Kirkes as substances 'produced by one tissue or organ to which some other portion of the body has been biologically adapted to such an extent that its normal function can proceed only under the influence of the substance.' The more important organs which, according to modern views, produce internal secretions are the Thyroid, Parathyroid, Pituitary, Thymus, Suprarenals, and Chromaffin Tissues, the Pancreas, the Duodenal and Pyloric Mucosa, the Liver, Kidney, Testis, Ovary, Corpus Luteum, Placenta and Foetus. These substances are definite, but complex, chemical bodies and differ from the enzymes in being thermostable.   By these enzymes we mean the external secretions, such as diastase, pepsin, typsin, etc., elaborated by the digestive organs. The function of the Internal Secretions seems to be to provoke the manufacture of enzymes and to promote their action, and generally to act as excitants to physiologic activity.

"The Hormones which definitely have been proved to exist are: the pancreatic secretion, formed in the epithelium of the duodenal mucous membrane, which stimulates the flow of pancreatic juice; a Hormone formed in the pancreas which influences the absorptive activity of the intestinal epithelium; the gastric

secretin formed in the pyloric mucosa, which
stimulates the secretion of gastric juice; vaso-
dilator Hormones formed in functionally active
tissue which have a specific effect upon the,
vessels of the functioning organ; a vaso-constricting and diuretic Hormone secreted in the
posterior lobe of the pituitary body; another
vaso-constricting Hormone in the kidneys; a
Hormone produced in the anterior lobe of the
pituitary body, determining the growth of bone
and connective tissue; a Hormone controlling
the oxidation of sugar and manufactured in the
pancreas; a thymus Hormone which influences
the development of the reproductive organs;
a Hormone produced by the salivary glands
which controls the flow of water from the
blood capillaries in these glands; a foetal Hormone which stimulates the growth of the mammary glands; ovarian and testicular Hormones
which have to do with the processes of reproduction. * * *

"The subject of the Internal Secretions is
one of no little intricacy. A deficiency or an
excess of one or several of these secretions, it
will be seen, may upset the whole chemical
balance of metabolism. Indeed, without certain of these secretions the body cannot live.
* * * The action of the Internal Secretions is
complex and as yet imperfectly understood.
Many facts, however, have been collated from
experimental observations which throw consid-

erable light upon this obscure subject. Some of these observations illustrate the manner in which Hormone balance is preserved. * * * *"

The Therapeutic Value of the Internal Secretions. In modern medicine there is found frequent reference to what is called "Organotherapy," or "Opotheraphy," which terms are employed to indicate "the use of animal organs, their extracts or active principles, as medicines." As we have stated in the preceding pages, the extract of the several Ductless Glands are now being employed extensively in the treatment of certain diseases, particularly those diseases which are held to result from a deficiency of the particular internal secretion in question.

Modern Organotherapy usually is held to have begun with Brown-Sequard, although, in 1850, Berthold began a serious investigation of the Internal Secretions of the Ductless Glands, followed shortly after by those of Claude Berpard. Brown-Sequard advanced as his basic principle the following axiomatic statement: "All glands of the body, whether they are excretory canals or not, give to the blood useful principles, the absence of which is felt when the glands are extirpated or destroyed by disease." Subsequent investigations and observations have tended to corroborate the Brown-Sequard basic principle.

The New International Encyclopaedia, in its article upon Organotherapy, says: "Almost every gland and tissue in the body has been studied experimentally, and several substances· of unique value have been added to our therapeutic resources, e.g., adrenaline, thyroid extract, and pituitary extract. To a large extent, however, Organotherapy still rests upon an empirical basis, and this for several reasons: some of these glands have more than one active principle; similar physiological effects are produced by several glands; antagonisms are observed between certain glands and even parts of the same gland, and it is difficult to analyze the symptoms calling for a particular principle; there is a great difficulty in securing active preparations, many of those on the market being inert; and, finally, there is undoubtedly a subtle, vital difference between animal extracts and their human equivalent. By many writers these active principles are considered as chemical entities which they term Hormones, typical examples of which are secretin, adrenaline, and thyroid extract. * * * * Animal extracts should be prepared from adult healthy normal animals. Those preferably selected are sheep and hogs. Gland tissues are no longer given raw. The thyroid gland has been transplanted into cretins with some degree of success. Many different preparations have been made, among which may be mentioned glycerin extracts, watery extracts, the dried and powdered gland, and compressed tablets. Some glandular principles are inactive when given by the mouth, and must be injected hypodermically to secure their physiological effects."

The foregoing consideration of the Ductless Glands and their Internal Secretions, including the subject of the therapeutic employment of the active principles and extracts of these secretions, logically leads us to the consideration of the physiological functions and offices of those Ductless Glands (for they are undoubtedly such) known as the Genital Glands, i.e., the Testes and the Ovaries, respectively; and to the consideration of the therapeutic employment of the principles of such in the treatment of diseased conditions. This new phase of the subject is intensely interesting, and extremely instructive, and has a most direct bearing upon the general subject of Regeneration which is the subject-matter of this book. In the next following section of this book this new phase of the subject is considered in detail.

VI

OFFICES OF THE GENITAL GLANDS,

One of the important results of the investigations of the Ductless Glands which have occupied the attention of advanced physiologists of recent years, and one which has been combatted by certain of the more orthodox physiologists for some reason, is the discovery that the Genital Glands are true Ductless Glands manifesting internal secretions of certain substances apart from those primarily concerned with the primary reproductive processes. This discovery has afforded a scientific explanation of the facts which for ages have been asserted by the occultists and other heterodox thinkers, i.e., the facts concerned with the processes of Regeneration.

In the preceding section of this book we have called your attention to the fact that there is a disposition on the part of certain ultra-conservative physiologists to question even the fact that the Genital Glands are true "glands" at all. These orthodox scientists strive to maintain the antiquated idea that the Genital Glands "are not in any true sense 'glands,' for they do not produce any chemical substances peculiar to themselves, but are simply the portions of the body where those cells are formed from which the next generation arises."

But, as you have probably noticed, these same ultra-conservative scientists quite as earnestly maintain that "the use of the term 'gland' in connection with the suprarenal capsules, the pituitary body, and the pineal body, is incorrect and confusing." This, notwithstanding the fact that Science has not only discovered the truth that these Ductless Glands undoubtedly do manifest important internal secretions; that such secretions have been widely and successfully employed in therapeutic practice; and that the physiological effect of such secretions upon the physical processes have been definitely determined by experiment.

Advanced modern physiology has at least tentatively advanced the theory that the Genital Glands, particularly the Testes and the Ovaries, not only produce the primary reproductive cells, but that they also secrete other substances of a high potency which are believed to exert a strong influence not only upon the growth and development of the embryo after the ovum has been fertilized by the sperm, but also upon the growth and development of the body of the individual in whose Genital Glands they have been secreted.

The Testes and the Ovaries are found to manifest true internal secretions of this kind,

which secretions meet the requirements of
Internal Secretions which are stated as follows: "Internal Secretions are substances elaborated in Ductless Glands and discharged di-.
rectly into the blood; they are substances secreted by animal organs or tissues which preside over the development, growth, reproduction, and the chemical regulation of the body."

In Section IV of this book we have called
your attention to quotations from several
authorities which express the belief of such
thinkers and investigators that the internal
secretions of the Genital Glands are discharged
into the blood, thereafter to perform certain
important offices in the growth, development,
and vital processes of the individual.

For instance, these authorities says that: "It
goes back into the circulation ready to form
the finest brain, nerve, and muscular tissue";
and, "The unexpended sexual energy is employed for the building up of a keener brain,
and more vital and enduring nerves and
muscles"; and, "The sexual glands are useful
for the physical well-being of the individual,
through the vital stimulus exercised by them
through their peculiar secretion upon the processes of development and nutrition"; and,
"The seminal secretion has a wonderfully immanent value, and if retained is absorbed into
the system and adds enormously to man's magnetic, mental, and spiritual force"; and, "The

sexual energies may be transferred to the other departments, to which they contribute largely in the life and power of each, and in the production of general vigor"; and, "The sexual department of a continent adult seems to be a sort of storage battery of vitality, a veritable reservoir for surplus energy."

In addition to these positive statements, the following quotations will serve to illustrate the strong and rapidly spreading belief along these lines among thoughtful scientific investigators and observers. Professor Kingsley says: "The interstitial cells carry secretions in men which pass into the blood. They apparently cause secondary male characteristics such as, among other things, hair on the face and change of voice at the close of boyhood. They also govern most female characteristics." Professor Keith says: "The interstitial gland has as much to do with the growth, in certain particulars, as the pituitary gland has in general bodily growth. All the changes we see in children after they begin to grow, which bring to prominence racial characteristics, depend upon the action of the interstitial gland. If the gland is removed, or remains in abeyance, the maturing of the body is prolonged or altered."

The effect upon the physical and mental characteristics of the lower animals, and of men and women, which is produced by disease of or the removal of the Genital Glands is so striking that it is impossible to escape the conviction that these glands internally secrete substances which are appropriated by the blood and which directly affect the physical and mental condition of the individual.

For instance, all are familiar with the changed mental and physical condition of the cock transformed into a capon; of the young stallion transformed into a gelding; of the young bull transformed into a steer; of the normal human male transformed into a eunuch;—the transformation in each of these cases being caused by the removal of the male Genital Glands. The transformation is followed by marked physical and mental changes. The body loses its male characteristics, and tends to become sluggish, heavy, slow; the eyes lose their sparkle, the voice changes its character; courage is lost and ambition disappears; inertia and docility are manifested. There is a general "heaviness" of body, mind, and emotional nature. A similar mental and physical change is manifested in female animals, and in women, who have been deprived of their ovaries.

It has been noted that the seed of plants and of animals are composed of a highly concentrated food substance, this in some cases being also true of the outer covering surrounding the seed proper. This is Nature's provision for supplying the developing young life-form with highly concentrated food-material until it is able to draw its supply of food from outside sources. Man instinctively recognizes the high food-value of such material when he seeks and finds an important part of his food supply in the seed substances of plants and animals. In nuts, fruit, berries, grain, and in eggs, he finds this valuable seed-substance. This substance is supplied by the action of the secretions of the Genital Glands or sex-cells of animal or plant, and such office is undoubtedly a part of the varied functions of the sexual organism. Moreover, there is evidently "something more" in milk than the ordinary food materials contained in it.

The above, and many other discovered facts, have gradually led thoughtful investigators and observers to the conclusion that in the Genital Glands of animals and men there are secreted powerful and subtle chemical elements which are, in part at least, absorbed into the blood and thence carried to all parts of the system, there serving to energize, invigorate and strengthen the cells, organs, and parts of the body—including the brain and nervous system. Some have gone so far as to hazard the opinion that old age is chiefly due to the lessening of the supply of these secretions. From general hypothesis to particular theory, this thought has proceeded; and then, as usual, the special theory has sought expression, manifestation, and exemplification in actual experiment.

It was the natural, logical evolution of this thought which caused the early investigators among modern scientists to arrive at the conclusion that, if the Genital Glands actually do produce these internal secretions, then if these secretions could be introduced artificially into the system there should result a marked and definite physiological change. This was accompanied by the belief that certain abnormal physical conditions caused by a deficiency of such secretions might be remedied by the supplying of the particular elements contained in them. From this basic position the experiments of the early investigators proceeded.

Brown-Sequard was the pioneer in this experimental work, although he was aided by the earlier investigations of Berthold and Bernard. Brown-Sequard, an eminent physiologist, the professor of experimental medicine at the College de France, in the year 1889, announced the startling results of certain experiments conducted by him over a period of several years. He started with the basic hypothesis that: "All glands of the body, whether they are excretory canals or not, give to the blood useful principles, the absence of which is felt when the glands are extirpated or destroyed by disease."

Upon this basis, he reasoned that from his experiments he had demonstrated conclusively that human life, and physical and mental vigor, could be prolonged by means of the administering of a hypodermic injection of a fluid extract in which the testicles of sheep had been macerated: this extract being the afterward famous "Brown-Sequard Elixir." The value of this discovery, and the reputation of the discovery, were seriously affected by the sensational announcements of the newspapers concerning the "Elixir of Life," and by the ridicule and abuse which came as the result of the reaction of the disappointed general public who had been lead to expect a miracle—the boon of Eternal Youth and Physical Immortality.

This unfortunate reaction, and the resulting ridicule, operated so as to bring disfavor upon the discovery and the experiments which had led to them: the real merits of the theory and experiments were lost sight of for a long time. Later, however, interest in the discovery was reawakened by new experiments which served to substantiate them, and at present Brown-Sequard is regarded as a pioneer in the now important branch of medical theory and practice. A leading reference work says of him and his work: "Recent experiments serve to substantiate the views and statements of Brown-Sequard. His famous Elixir, consisting of an extract of lamb's testicles, he administered to himself, and reported marvelous stimulating and rejuvenating effects. While other observers failed to substantiate his somewhat extravagant assertions, it was recognized that there undoubtedly existed a powerful oxidizing and stimulating element in these organs, and physiologists were led into wider fields of investigation."

Science has not as yet determined the exact way in which the internal secretions of the genital glands produce general physical and mental changes in the individual, but the following quotations from authoritative reference works will serve to indicate the general direction of scientific thought on the subject:

"It is known that several, perhaps very many, if not all glands have also the power of secreting substances to which Starling has given the name of 'hormones.' These pass into the blood and cause other glands to secrete. Thus, an acid in the duodenum causes it to secrete a hormone to which the name of 'secretin' is given. This passes to the pancreas and causes increased secretion from that gland. It is probable that the pancreas, in turn, also secretes something which activates a ferment in the muscles. It is evident therefore that the connection between the different glands of the body is a very complicated one, and that the effects of a drug which acts upon

any one of them may be of a very far-reaching
character. It is by no means impossible that
all glands have a double or even triple function,
and that sometimes the external may be even
less important than the internal secretion. On
this point, however, we have but little definite
knowledge, and a great field is open for future
research. At the same time, there are many
indications of the importance of an internal
secretion in popular treatment. * * * It now
seems probable that all glands which have
what may be termed an external secretion
. . . . have also an internal secretion, so that
while they are pouring out one secretion from
the ducts into the intestine or external air, they
are also pouring into the lymphatics, and thus
into the blood, an internal secretion. In fact,
a splitting appears to take place in the process
of secretion somewhat resembling that which
takes place in the formation of a toxin and
anti-toxin."

Another authoritative reference work gives
the following interesting statement concerning
the mutual affinity of certain secretions for certain other glands, and of the mutual antag-
onism observed to exist between others:

"The Suprarenal Glands have been shown to
be stimulated by, and to work in harmony
with, the Thyroid and Pituitary; they antag-
onize the Pancreas, especially in the control of
sugar secretion; they inhibit the Thymus and

Secretin, and stimulate the Testic and Ovary. The Thyroid stimulates and is stimulated by the Reproductive Glands, co-operates with the Hypophysis, stumulates the Adrenals, and in-hibits the Pancreas. Thyroid secretion in excess stimulates the Intestines. The posterior lobe of the Hypophysis stimulates the smooth muscle of the Uterus and Intestines, co-operates with the Thyroid, stimulates the Mammae, and is antagonized by the Ovary and Pineal Body. There is said to be an antagnostic action between it and the Pancreas. The Pancreas controls and is controlled by the Adrenals, and is assisted by the Parathyroids; it is stimulated by the secretion formed in the Duodenal Mucosa, and is apparently inhibited by the Thyroid and the Hypophysis. The Spleen is believed to have a stimulating influence upon the Stomach and digestion generally, and to furnish a stimulant to the muscles of the Intestines. When to these actions and cross-actions are added those of the Reproductive Glands, the Pineal Body, the Thymus, Parathyroids, Mammae, and Liver, it will be appreciated that the subject of the Internal Secretions is one of no little delicacy."

One of the most significant hints along these lines so far offered by Science is that in which is pointed out the close affinity existing between the Genital Glands and the Thyroid Glands. Again, in this connection, may be pointed out the close affinity between the Brain and the Genital Organism, on the one hand; and the close affinity existing between the Brain and the Thyroid, on the other hand. Here we seem to have a triangle of sympathetic action, or affinity of process: the three respective sides being represented by (1) the Brain, (2) the Thyroid, and (3) the Genitals, respectively.

We need not dwell here upon the close affinity between Brain and Genital Glands, or upon their action and reaction—this is too well known to require extended discussion. You know that excessive mental work will weaken the genital powers; and that excessive sexual activity will weaken the brain action: these are matters of common knowledge and general experience, needing no elaboration or argument.

As for the other phases of the triangular affinity, we may refer, in the first place, to the well-established relation between the Thyroid and the Genital Organism; and, in the second place, to the result of deficiency in the Thyroid secretions in the direction of producing impaired Brain action and even idiocy. Treatment of mental weakness by means of Thyroid extract has proved quite successful. There is here seen to be a close relation of Brain, Thyroid, and Genital Glands.

An authoritative reference work says: "Under the influence of Thyroid Gland these symptoms (those of myxoedema) disappear, and the patient is frequently restored to a normal condition. When the Thyroid Gland is absent in children, not only is the expression . of the face dull and heavy as in the adult, but the growth both of body and mind is arrested, and the child remains a stunted idiot. The effect of the administering of Thyroid Gland in such cases is marvelous, the child growing in body and becoming healthy and intelligent. In the case of the Thyroid the function of the gland appears to be to prepare a secretion which is poured out into the blood and alters tissue-changes."

Whatever may be the true and final explanation, however, it is a fact proved by many experiments that extracts prepared from the secretions of the Genital Organs frequently produce marvelous physiological and psychological changes in the organism into which they are injected or otherwise administered. Since the time of Brown-Sequard there have been many earnest investigators and experimentors along these lines, publicity being avoided, however, for obvious reasons since the unfortunate Brown-Sequard experience. There have been many cases reported in medical journals of the reinvigorating effect of administered extracts of Testes or of Ova.

A reference work conservatively states: "Of the reproductive glands, orchitic (testicular) extract, while not enjoying much favor, has been shown to promote oxidation in the body, and has been given with varying results in hysteria, neurasthenia, locomotor ataxia, epilepsy, and insanity. Ovarian extract is similar in its action, though less powerful. An intensified effect is obtained from extract of the corpus luteum. These substances have been used in chlorosis, in the nervous disturbances following oophorectomy, and during the menapause. Great caution is advised in their use."

However, the most striking proofs of the effects produced upon the general physical and mental being of the individual by the action of the internal secretions of the Genital Glands are those which have been furnished during the past few years by the surgical experimentors along the lines of "Gland Transplantation" in animals and in human beings. The records of this phase of modern advanced surgery read like fairy-tales, and the leading practitioners in this branch of therapeutics run a great danger of suffering as did Brown-Sequard by reason of sensational newspaper reports, and the subsequent reaction of a disappointed general public. The public is being led to expect miracles, and is likely to become indignant when it is told that the whole subject is still merely in the experimental stage, and that Nature's rigid laws still are operative.

VII

GLAND TRANSPLANTATION

We shall now ask you to consider the plain, actual facts of "Genital Gland Transplantation" as reported in serious scientific works, and which are now receiving extended notice on the part of the scientific reviews and similar publications. Ignoring the fantastic reports which have already been begun by certain more or less sensational newspapers, the facts of the case as they are reported by the serious and careful scientific publications are substantially as follows:

Steinach, an eminent Viennese surgeon, startled the scientific world several years ago by announcing that he had succeeded in transforming male animals into females, and vice-versa. His experiments were conducted upon small animals, generally upon rats and guinea-pigs, and consisted of the transplanting of the Genital Glands from the animal of one sex to the body of the animal of the opposite sex. The rats or guinea pigs were first castrated, and then the ovaries or testes (as the case might be) were transplanted, or implanted.

When the operation was successful, the animal subsequently lost its original second-

110

ary sexual characteristics and assumed those corresponding to the sex-character of the implanted gland. Thus, the males became females, and the females became males, so far as their secondary sex characteristics were concerned; when the operations were failures, the animals became neuters manifesting no special secondary sex characteristics.

Steinach, as the result of these experiments, announced his theory that the differences in secondary sex characteristics between male and female arise not from the anatomical character of the sex organs, but rather from the secretions of certain genital cells. These cells, called Leydig cells, or Lutein cells, were found to manifest a secretion which determines the secondary sexual characteristics of the animal. "These cells," said Steinach, "are really glands." These secretions of the transplanted glands developed feminine physical form and mental and emotional characteristics in the female animal, and masculine physical form, and mental and emotional characteristics, in the female animal.

But this, important as it was in itself, was but the beginning of Steinach's startling discoveries. He also found that upon the state and activity of these sexual glands depended largely the health, vigor, and general vitality of the individual animal. His series of experiments proved this beyond question. Steinach found that individual animals were often much younger than their age would indicate, or much older; investigation revealed a direct connection between this youthfulness or "oldness", and the state and condition of these particular glands. This was found true concerning both males and females.

Steinach then came to the conclusion that it might be possible to give new youth to an old animal by supplying him with new Genital Glands. So he began to experiment upon old rats for this purpose. The aged male rat is marked by a coarse, bristly coat, falling out of the hair, sinking of the head, excessive curvature of the back, loss of weight, weakness of muscle, and similar signs of senility; his pugnacity disappears, his eyes blink, his face assumes a stupid expression, and he apparently loses all interest in life.

By means of Roentgen rays, ligatures of the Genital Glands and by the grafting of the Genital Glands of young rats upon old ones, Steinach obtained the almost miraculous result of transforming their advanced senility into youthful vigor and energy. The once old rats became young in every way. They assumed a youthful contour and form, and manifested youthful physical and mental, as well as emotional characteristics.

The experiments have now proceeded so far that the "old rats made young," again growing old by the passage of time, have been "made young" for the second time, and with the same remarkable results. How long this process of repeated renewal of youth may be continued remains for time to decide—the experiments are too recent to allow of this question being decided.

A general and popular account of the Steinach experiments appeared in "The Literary Digest," published November 20, 1920; from which the following is culled:

"A man named Steinach, in Vienna, has been experimenting for ten years with rats. Full accounts of his work were published last summer in the great biological journal founded by Roux, and these were summarized and discussed by the 'London Athenaeum,' which is now the most interesting of all English weeklies. It is from the 'Athanaeum's' account that I am taking these facts. Steinach has been studying the interstitial cells that fill in the spaces between the tubules of the testes in males, and between the follicles of the ovaries in females. His reason for choosing these cells for his experiments is that they are a wellspring of life. Furthermore, since all our vital functions are interrelated, to make these cells active gives the whole organism new life and strength. This is not the only way of stimulating the organism, but it seems the most powerful.

"An old rat is like a senile old man; he is bald and emaciated, his eyes are clouded, his breathing is labored. He stays in one place, with bent back, and has small interest in anything. If you cut (or ligate?) one of his genital ducts, however, which is a comparatively slight operation, it has the effect of making the interstitial cells multiply actively. Waves of life flood his being. Within a few weeks he is transformed. These currents restore and rebuild him; skin, muscle and mind. Both in looks and behavior he is indistinguishable from other strong rats. He has cast off old age. Senility begins after twenty or thirty months in a rat. He is then about through. But when an operation is performed on a senile rat he gets from six to eight months' new life. In other words, the addition to his normal span is 20 to 30 per cent. The rat lives it vigorously, eagerly, back to his prime. When senility again comes upon him it is in a modified form. His organism as a whole is in better shape. It is his mind now that tires. As Steinach has already cut (or ligated?) one or both of his genital ducts, that method of stimulating his cells cannot, of course, be repeated. But another operation is ready. Some unfortunate young male is deprived of his testes by Steinach, and these are implanted forthwith in this hoary old rat. A second spell of active life follows, not so long as the first. It ends in acute psychic senility. The rat goes all to pieces. It is as if the brain, twice restimulated to emotion, curiosity, keenness, had approached the very limit of its running, and was completely exhausted.

"Steinach has not as yet tried whether a third rejuvenation is possible. That remains to be seen. He lives in Vienna, and everything there has come to a stop. He has no assistants, no funds, with which to conduct further experiments. 'May happier lands or cities carry the work on,' he writes at the end. Steinach has naturally found it more difficult to give new youth to females. But here, too, he has in a measure succeeded. X-Ray treatment and ovarian transplantation are the methods employed. As to human experiments, there is a colleague of Steinach's named Lichtenstern, who has operated on numerous men and women with apparent success. There has not been time yet to measure how long their new lease of life is to be; but they have regained the joy of life they had lost—strength and powers of work. Still, all this needs confirming."

In "Current Opinion" for January, 1921, there appeared a general mention of the work of Steinach, based upon an article in the "Illustrirte Zeitung" written by Dr. Erich Ebsteain, who apparently confirms the reports of the success of the Steinach experiments. The article in question contains the following interesting statements:

"These cells are really glands. Whether an individual be in a state of vigor or debility depends upon the state of these glands. Sometimes we see a person advanced in years who has more strength and more vitality than one of half his age. The difference is due to the state of the glands to which Steinach thus directs attention. Steinach asked himself if it were possible, through a special treatment of these glands, to renew the vigor of youth in the aged or in the debilitated. The thing called youth may be the effect of the freshness of these glands. * * * * A little over two years ago Steinach encouraged two of his pupils to undertake the surgery of rejuvenation upon human objects. The results were in many instances no less remarkable than those obtained with rats. There was a renewal of physical vigor, a diminution of the trembling of the hands, a finer bearing, more alertness mentally.

"It was observed that the rates thus operated on had their lives prolonged considerably beyond the normal longevity for their species. How long these effects may endure in the case of human beings is yet to be determined, because this form of surgery is of too recent origin to draw sweeping inferences. Certain it is that the gland surgery practiced upon the rat attains results no less striking when applied to aged men and aged women. Repeated experiments seem to confirm the theory of Steinach that sex characteristics do not reside where they have hitherto been assumed to reside, but in the glands which give forth a secretion known by the name of Boux, after the brilliant physiologist whose theories first gave Steinach his clue."

While Steinach and his students have been conducting experiments along the lines above indicated, there have been others in Europe and America who have been making similar experiments, and who have evolved from the original experiments upon the lower animals to such an extent that they are now performing similar operations upon human individuals, with,at least in many cases, quite remarkable results, so far as the reports indicate. We shall now ask you to consider in brief outline the nature and results of such experiments and lines of treatment; for, apart from their own general interest and importance, these have a direct bearing upon the subject of Regeneration by methods entirely different from their own—psychological methods, not surgical op- .erations. The physiological principle, however, is the same in both forms of treatment or procedure.

It is somewhat difficult to obtain definite details concerning the experiments now being conducted by a number of surgeons in Europe and the United States in the direction of the transplanting of the Genital Glands of animals into the bodies of men and women. This difficulty arises from several causes, among which the principal are (1) the observance of professional ethics in the matter of sensational reports partaking of the nature of advertising; (2) the fear of sensational newspaper reports, highly seasoned, and almost invariably followed by the reaction of the popular mind accompanied by ridicule and abuse, and (3) the reluctance of the patient concerning public notoriety which is usually accompanied by ridicule, adverse comment, and mistaken estimates of the causes leading the patient to undergo such an operation.

The last named cause is particularly effective in preventing publicity. The popular mind, hearing of operations of this kind, seems to jump to the conclusion that the patient has undergone the operation for the purpose of regaining lost sexual power, or for strengthening weak sexual power—"sexual power" being construed as meaning the power to indulge in the sexual act with a marked degree of frequency and repetition. This last conception, coupled with the fact that goats' glands are usually employed in the transplantation, the goat being commonly known as an abnormally lustful animal. causes a derisive and scornful comment and criticism which the average man or woman dreads and shuns.

The injustice of criticism of this kind is particularly marked in this case, for the reason that the operation is usually undertaken not for the purpose of obtaining increase of the power to indulge frequently in the sexual act, but rather for the cure of general debility, nervous prostration, premature senility, and similar complaints. Moreover, the surgeons performing this class of operations almost invariably caution their patients against subsequent excessive sexual indulgence, and preach most vigorously the doctrine of the Conservation of the Life Forces imminent in the sexual-gland secretions. Their instructions to the patient, and the treatment itself, are based upon the principle that the vital fluids generated in the male and female Genital Glands (the Testes and the Ovaries), which are not expended in the reproductive processes, are taken up by the blood and are then absorbed by the various tissues of the body—strength, health, vigor, and improved functioning power thus being imparted to them.

Indeed, in many cases the surgeons have employed certain methods well known to physicians to restrain the reinvigorated man from sexual indulgence for at least a year following the operation, in order that he may conserve and receive the benefit of the reabsorbed internal secretions of the Genital Glands which had been stimulated into renewed activity by the operation. These surgeons vary this practice only in exceptional cases in which offspring are desired by the reinvigorated patient. It is generally held by the surgeons practicing this method that overindulgence in the sexual act, following the reinvigoration caused by the implantation of the goat's glands, will defeat and nullify the benefits which normally arise from the increased stimulation. "Conservation and Regeneration" is the slogan of these practitioners.

The transplanting operation, however, is reported as having been quite successful in the cure of sterility of both man and woman. This, of course, means nothing more than increased generative power, and not Regenerative Power in general. More important, therefore, are the numerous reported cases of marked cures effected by the transplantation of the Genital Glands in cases of nervous prostration, general debility, feeble mentality, insanity, dementia praecox, locomotor ataxia, mental depression, melancholia, prostatitis, hardening of the arteries, high blood-pressure, failing eyesight, vertigo, defective hearing and deafness, chronic constipation, chronic skin diseases, eczema, psoriasis, senility, etc., and of "general breakdown."

It is claimed that in many cases the patients undergoing the transplantation operation become rejuvenated in physical appearance, their eyes becoming brighter, their skin clearer and softer, and their carriage and walk becoming like those of much younger persons. Hardened arteries are reported to have been transformed into normal condition and functioning, and high blood-pressure to have disappeared. In some cases, women who had passed the Menopause stage of life have had a return of the menstrual flow. In short, these men and women seem to have responded to the treatment just as did Steinach's rats and guinea-pigs—they have "taken on a new lease of life."

Of course, it is too early to determine just how long this renewed youth and vigor will continue, or whether it may again be renewed when age again makes its appearance; but cases treated three or four years ago are said to show no sign of a relapse, or of a loss of their renewed vitality. Some have estimated the probable continuance of the effect of the transplanting at about fifteen years, and they hold that the experiments upon animals justify the hope of the successful renewal of the effect by a second operation at the end of that time. These advanced experimenters dream of the increase of man's normal life from the proverbial "three-score-and-ten" to at least twice that number of years—but this realization belongs to the future, and is but tentative conjecture at the present time.

The gland-transplantation is usually effected by implanting the Genital Gland of a young male goat into the body of the man; and the Genital Glands of a young female goat into the woman; the transplanting being performed within a few minutes after the removal of the glands from the living goats. Sometimes the whole gland is implanted; again only a portion. Women are reported as responding to the treatment even more rapidly and more decidedly than men, so far as is concerned the return of youthful physical appearance, youthful spirits, and youthful mental vigor.

The following selected quotations from an article appearing in "The New York American," of March 14, 1920, will furnish some further interesting information concerning the details of this form of surgical treatment. The article in question contains an interview with Dr. J. R. Brinkley, an American surgeon, who has performed a number of these operations during the past several years. Dr. Brinkley is reported as saying:

"Where substitution of glands of any character is essential, they should be taken from the goat operated upon immediately before the human implanting, and be inserted at once. Glands should not be taken from the ape or other animals for human use. The goat is immune to tuberculosis. He is a clean animal, full of health and vitality. Apes are very subject to tuberculosis. One can never tell whether or not an ape is entirely free from disease. It is generally unlawful to substitute our human glands, and, even though they could be readily obtained, they are apt to be infected with some disease. * * *

"The goat alone among mammals reacts to poisons almost identically as human beings react, and the poison gases of the war had precisely the same effect upon him as upon the soldiers. So 1,500 goats did their bit in the war in an experimental way. These points in his favor, and other similarities to man, are the reasons which led me to select the goat as the best possible material in this work. Goatglands alone seem to be harmonious and sympathetic when transplanted into the human body. In other words, the hormones of goat and man agree. We still know less about the causes of hormones than the effects. On account of the mutual tolerance of goat and human hormones, the goat gland speedily attaches a blood supply in the human body, and cell by cell is replaced so that it soon functions as the original gland would had it been present and normal. * * *

"I have named the process 're-creative gland operation' in accordance with the belief now general among genetists and anatomists that if the clock of time is ever to be turned back for humanity it can be only through glandular transplantations. Glands have proved much superior to any animal extract or serum in this class of cases. Often in serums the poison elements are retained, but not the nutritive. We use the whole goat gland, as a rule, because we do not know in what part of it the hormones hide. The attempted transplantation of kidneys have thus far failed, because the kidney product is waste matter, not live cells as in the case of the interstitial glands."

We have directed your attention to the foregoing reports of the Steinach experiments, and those of the operation of gland transplantation upon human beings, merely for the purpose of illustrating and proving the modern interest in the subject on the part of scientific investigators, and the existence of a scientific basis for the general principle of Regeneration. These experiments undoubtedly are of great importance in the field of scientific research along the lines of the determination of the offices of the Ductless Glands, the internal secretions, the hormones, etc., as well as along those of the nature of the derivative offices and functions of the sexual organism. Moreover, these experiments seemingly indicate the opening of a new and important branch of surgical practice, and practical therapy.

But with such matters, important though they may be in their own field, we have no immediate concern in this inquiry into the principles of Regeneration. Having employed these reports as illustrations of a general principle, we may now be permitted to pass beyond them in our general inquiry. We believe that the average human being is able to increase, develop, and manifest his Regenerative Power by purely psychological methods; however, these methods bring actively into play the purely physiological processes of the body.

While in exceptional cases the individual may be justified in seeking medical or surgical methods of developing Regenerative Power—of employing glandular extracts, or gland transplantation—we believe that in the great majority of cases the individual may accomplish the desired result, and obtain the hoped for effect, by the employment of the purely psychological methods to which we have referred, and which we shall now proceed to consider in detail in this inquiry and instruction.

VIII

THE SECRET OF REGENERATION

A careful analysis of the methods employed by the ancient sages and their followers in the processes of Regeneration, and an equally careful analysis of the methods employed by the modern scientific experimenters along the same general lines, reveals the presence of a common underlying principle of applying and directing the regenerative forces of the Sex Energy of the individual.

This common underlying principle of application and direction is found to consist of the awakening and arousing of the subtle elements of the internal secretions of the Genital Glands, and the direction of their energies into the channels of the general invigoration, stimulation, and vitalization of the various glands, organs, and nerve-centres of the entire physical organism. The invigoration, stimulation and vitalization of the brain result in an increase of mental efficiency; the invigoration, stimulation and vitalization of the other physical centres result in an increase of physical efficiency, health, and vigor.

The careful investigator of the phenomena of Regeneration, if he be well informed concerning the subject of the effect and influence of the psychological factors upon the physical factors of the human organism, soon discovers that the ancient teachers of Regeneration called into activity and effect these psychological factors, which, in turn, brought into action and effect the physical factors. Likewise, the modern scientific experimenters, while calling into action and effect the purely physical factors, also have brought into action and effect the purely psychological factors.

This joint and coordinated action and effect is produced by each of these different classes of experimenters and investigators, notwithstanding the fact that each class seemingly overlooks the particular factor which is not emphasized in its own theory and practice, and notwithstanding the fact that each class attributes the obtained result to the presence and activity of the particular factor which is especially emphasized in its own theory and teaching. You will see how this has worked out as we now proceed to consider the respective theories of these different classes of investigators and experimenters.

The ancient sages, and the teachers of the esoteric schools, believed that the Sex Energy is an immaterial energy abiding in the physical organism, just as electricity or magnetism abides in physical substances. They knew nothing of "internal secretions," or "hormones," or of the chemical organic substances in which the regenerative force of Nature abides. They were right so far as their knowledge extended, but their knowledge of physical processes did not go far enough. They discovered that these subtle energies of the body may be called into activity, and directed into action, by means of the exercise of thought and will. Here again they were right concerning the main facts, though ignorant of the intermediate stage of the processes employed.

Not knowing anything of the physical regenerative factors, they never dreamt of producing Regeneration in the lower animals; and for that matter, the minds of the animals not being capable of being appealed to, or set into operation, their methods would have been without effect in such cases. Their entire attention was fixed upon the psychological processes involved in the manifestation of Regeneration, and these processes seemed to them to have no logical or natural relation to those processes which they recognized as being purely physical.

The modern, scientific investigators and experimenters, on the contrary, recognize only the purely physical factors involved in their experiments and the results of these; the psychological factors involved being practically ignored by them. They are strengthened in this mental attitude by the fact that the same class of results are obtained in the experiments upon the lower animals, in which the psychological element is clearly absent. To them, the entire process is of a chemico-physiological character. They recognize the existence of certain subtle, potent chemical substances secreted by the organism, and they perceive the effect upon the general physical system of the stimulation and increase of these secretions. The chemico-physiological explanation is sufficient to account for the results, and they see no need of looking for a further explanation in psychology.

But, in spite of this, the psychological factor is present and operative, at least to some extent, in all cases in which the subject of the experiment is a human being having a knowledge of, or at least a suspicion of, the object sought to be obtained by the experiment. The element of Suggestion enters into the equation, even though it be not invited; and where Suggestion is present and active, there the powers of the Subconscious (or Unconscious) Mentality are active in the direction of producing results and effects. Just as, in a similar way, Suggestion causes an increased secretion in many other glands of the human body, so does it increase the secretion of the Genital Glands; and just as the direction of the vital forces and processes is influenced by Suggestion, so is the direction of the Regenerative processes so influenced.

In other volumes of this series of books we have explained the part played by the Subconscious Mentality in the human physical economy. One phase of this plane of mentality presides over the vital and physiological processes, and exercises the power of law and order over them. The physical processes are not purely chemico-mechanical activities, but are directly under the influence and direction of the Subconscious Mentality, or "Unconscious Mind" as some have preferred to call it. Moreover, this Subconscious Mentality, or Unconscious Mind, which presides over the physical processes, is always more or less amenable to Suggestion and more or less under the possible direction of Will. The Thought and the Will of the individual are capable of producing either Disease or Health in his body, according to laws and principles now well understood and recognized by Science. Accordingly, the physiological processes involved in Regeneration may be, and often are, strongly influenced by the Thought and Will of the individual.

The foregoing facts logically lead the careful thinker to the conclusion that the methods of the modern scientific investigators and experimenters may be improved and rendered far more efficient by means of a definite and deliberate application of the principles of Psycho-

Therapy to the work of Regeneration, in addition to employment of the purely physical methods of the administration of the gland-extracts of Organotherapy or the implantation of the Genital Glands by means of a surgical operation. Such a thinker will be apt to decide that if, in addition to these physical methods, the patient is led through Suggestion or Auto-Suggestion, or similar methods of Psycho-Therapy, to "confidently expect" the efficient operation of the physical mechanism thus called into action, in the definite direction and manner which he has been led to visualize clearly and strongly, and to employ his will power persistently in the same special direction, then the work of the physician or surgeon will be rendered far more effective and certain.

But, be this as it may, it is not our purpose here to attempt to point out to the physician or surgeon the methods by means of which his particular system of setting into operation the processes of Regeneration may be improved and rendered more effective. Not only would he most naturally resent being thus advised in such a matter by a non-medical layman, and would probably be justified in reminding the ·latter of the virtue of the old proverbs which recite the advisability of "minding your own business," and which solemnly commands, "Shoemaker! Stick to your last!" but also, frankly, we are not here in the least concerned with the possible improvement of his methods, or the extension of his hypothesis.

Nor are we undertaking a propaganda in favor of the administration of gland-extracts, or of the gland implantation operation. Rather do we conceive the real purpose of our present consideration of the subject to be that of indicating the psychological methods whereby Regeneration may be effected and produced, and to point out how these methods may be improved and more efficiently applied than they were by the ancient teachers and their followers.

We believe that these ancient teachers and practitioners were essentially right in their general principles of application and method, although lacking in a complete theory concerning the fundamental principles involved in the process; and we believe that the fuller understanding concerning the chemico-physiological factors of the process, which has come to modern thinkers by reason of the researches, investigations and experiments of the scientific physiologists, will enable the modern psychotherapist to apply these old methods far more effectively, and in a more definite and positive form. The particulars of this improved method, and of the general theory underlying it, will form the subject of our instruction in the remaining pages of the present section of this book.

In the first place, modern psychology, particularly that phase of it which is concerned with the consideration of the influence of mental states upon physiological processes, furnishes the student with a wealth of illustrative material exemplifying the effect of emotional states upon the secretions of the body—upon the ordinary secretions and upon the internal secretions as well.

It is a matter of common knowledge that the secretion of the gastric and intestinal juices is largely augmented by the sight or even the thought and imaginative images of appetizing food. Actual experiments upon the lower animals have demonstrated that these digestive juices begin to be actively secreted by the animal when its favorite food is brought within its sight; and elaborate and ingenious experiments have shown that when the mind of a human being is filled with thoughts and imaginative images of appetizing food, then the secretion of such digestive fluids is largely increased.

Moreover, it is a matter of common experience among human beings that suggestions concerning delicious foods "make the mouth water," and cause the appetite to manifest itself; and that suggestions concerning the opposite class of substances result in producing feelings of nausea. The mere suggestion of sucking a lemon will cause an increased secretion and flow of saliva.

Again, the presence of the infant, or the sound of its hungry cry, will cause an increased secretion of milk within the mammary glands of the mother. It is also known that certain suggestions, thoughts, or emotions will tend to hasten the menstrual flow, while another class of emotions and suggestions will tend to retard it.

Certain strong emotions, particularly those of fright, will cause the secretion of chemical substances which will produce an evacuation of the bowels—an artificially induced diarrhea. Pleasant emotional states cause a flow of the digestive juices and promote the appetite; while unpleasant news, grief, worry and similar emotional states will cause one to lose all appetite for food.

Again, it has been proved that fear, anger, and especially jealousy, produce secretions which tend to poison the system; while cheerful, hopeful and inspiring mental states are seen to induce secretions which act as a physical tonic.

It is a matter of common experience, and of scientific record, that sad and depressing emotional states, long continued, tend to bring about a state of ill-health, lessened vitality, and even ultimate death; these physiological processes now being known to result directly from the presence and action of toxic secretions in the blood. On the other hand, it is as well known that the emotional states of successful love, certainty or strong hope of success in business or social undertakings, etc., will produce a marked improvement in the general health of the individual, in some cases almost "working a miracle" in his physical condition.

The effect of depressing emotions in the direction of inducing disease and retarding cure, and the effect of cheerful, inspiring emotions in the direction of maintaining or restoring health, are too well known to require extended argument to prove the action of the emotional states upon physiological conditions.

Finally, the effect of emotional states upon the sexual organism is well known to physicians, and recognized to at least some extent by the general public. That the sexual organism is aroused into activity and increased secretion by thoughts, mental images, and feelings of an amorous character is generally recognized. Indeed, in the case of young persons, physicians and moralists make a point of the importance of the avoidance of books, pictures, plays, and other suggestions which tend to arouse such feelings. There is on all sides the conviction that it is well "to keep the mind off such things." The artificial stimulation of the sexual nature by erotic literature, suggestive pictures, amatory plays, etc., is an established fact. That such things stimulate the sexual secretions is undoubted.

In the second place, modern psychology, especially those of its phases which are concerned with the effect and influence of "mind" or "thought" upon general health or disease, or upon their special phases or forms, teaches positively that the character of one's thoughts, fixed ideas, beliefs, and, above all, of his confident expectation, has a positive and decided effect upon the functioning of his physical organism. In fact, the whole structure of Mental Healing, Faith Cure, Suggestive Therapeutics, etc., rests upon the two principles of Therapeutic Psychology, or Psychological Therapeutics, which may be stated as follows: (1) the strong mental idea, thought, or mental picture of certain physical conditions, and (2) the confident expectation, lively hope, firm belief, or strong expectant attention directed toward the materialization or objectification of that idea, thought, or mental picture.

We do not deem it necessary to enter here upon an extended argument seeking to prove the truth of Mental Healing, or the Effect of the Mind upon the Body in the direction of producing Health or Disease. We feel warranted in assuming that you are sufficiently familiar with the accepted facts of the case, which are now known to most intelligent persons, to render needless any such extended argument or array of demonstrated facts. Psycho-Theraphy is now an established and well-recognized branch of medical science; and the reaction of Body to Mind is now an accepted fact of both modern physiology and modern psychology.

But, in spite of the general public knowledge concerning the effect of Mind upon Body, there is found a general disposition to overlook the fact that, although the mental states constitute the prime motive element of the physiological effect, yet there are present intermediate physiological processes and factors which are required to produce the result. Though the mental state of the patient sets into operation the recuperative and reparative processes of Nature in the body of the individual, these processes manifest along the established and normal lines of physiological functioning.

In many, if indeed not in all, of the "mental cures," the mind acts so as to set into activity the secretive functions of the various glands and organs, which acting upon the other glands, organs, and centres of the body bring about the restoration of normal health. The Mind is the prime, active agent; but it employs the mechanism and instruments of the physiological organism, among which the secretive processes hold a high rank. This fact is often overlooked by those who employ, and those

who are benefited by, the powers of Mental
Healing.

All this brings us down to the fact that in
the processes of Regeneration, by means of
which the general system is strengthened, reinvigorated, re-energized, by the forces and
energies inherent in the internal secretions of
the Genital Glands, there must be recognized
the presence and action of two factors, one
purely physiological, the other purely psychological.

The physiological factor, which is the only
one recognized by the medical practitioners
and surgeons treating and operating for the
purpose of inducing and producing Regeneration, is that which is concerned with the production of the internal secretions of the Genital
Glands, and their distribution to and their appropriation by the blood.

The psychological factor, which was the
only one recognized by the ancient sages, and
by many of their modern followers, is that
which is concerned with the action of the mental states upon the physiological functions and
activities—the employment of the Mind to set
into operation the "forces" or "energies" of the
Sex-Nature and to direct these to the general
physical system, including the brain.

If you have followed us carefully in the foregoing consideration of the subject, you will see
that our thought leads logically to the con-

clusion that the best and most effective methods to be employed in the processes of Regeneration are those methods which recognize and
manifest the following two principles: (1) the
existence of the special secretions of the Genital Glands which are designed for, and which
operate in the direction of, the promotion,
preservation and maintenance of the general
vigor, strength, and energy of the entire body;
and (2) the existence of certain powers of the
mind which are capable of calling into efficient
and effective activity the energies inherent in
these special secretions of the Genital Glands,
and of directing them to such parts of the body
which may require increased strength and
vitality, or to the entire physical system as a
whole.

You will also note that in this suggested
method, or methods, there are combined the
essential theory and facts both of the ancient
sages and teachers of Regeneration, and of the
modern scientific practitioners who are striving
to produce the manifestation of Regenerative
Power by means of the administration of gland-
extracts, or by gland implantation, or both,
The physiological facts are admitted and are
taken actively into consideration; the psychological activities and powers are employed under the guidance and direction of the mind,
thought, and will of the individual.

That the anicent sages and their followers obtained wonderful results in Regeneration by means of the practice of their general principles of application, i. e., the employment of the powers of the mind in the direction of arousing and distributing the Regenerative Power, cannot be denied. Many thousands have testified to the virtues and efficacy of their methods for many centuries, and their underlying principles constitute the essence of many schools of belief and practice at the present time. But, as all students of practical psychology must admit, the old sages lacked the clear visualization of the operation of the physiological processes which is now possible, and thereby were unable to employ the mental powers with the greatest efficiency—for a clear-cut, definite mental picture of the physical processes aids materially in its materialization. This deficiency is overcome by the combination-method now suggested.

Likewise, the modern scientific investigators and experimenters have produced wonderful results by means of the practice of their general principles of application, i. e., the introduction of the genital secretions into the system by the administration of gland-extracts or by the operation of gland implantation. But, as all students of Psycho-Therapy must admit, they have overlooked, or else discarded, the additional element of the Power of the Mind in the phases of Ideation, Visualization, and Volition, which would have enormously increased the efficacy of their methods. Their introduced secretions, if stimulated by the mind and directed by the will of the patient, would be far more effective than under the present system in which the psychological factors and elements of Regeneration are overlooked or ignored.

In this case, as in many others in all fields of human thought and work, the Secret is found in the reconcilation and harmonizing of the two principles which are apparently antithetically opposite to each other and having no common ground of identity or agreement, but which, at the last, are seen by the vision or Intuition to be really but the two polar extremes of the same general truth or principle —the two sides of the same shield.

IX

THE PRACTICE OF REGENERATION.

In the practice of Regeneration according to the methods of the ancient sages, modified by the discoveries of the later investigators of the subject, and employed in the light of the modern scientific knowledge concerning the nature of the internal secretions of the Genital Glands, the following three general principles are to be employed:

General Principles of Practice

(1) The employment of the psychological powers in the direction of the normal production of the internal secretions of the Genital Glands for the purposes of physical and mental reinvigoration, recuperation and revitalization; (2) The employment of the psychological powers in the direction of a sane and rational temperance in the matter of the expenditure of the sexual energies in the primary activities of the sex nature, and (3) the employment of the psychological powers in the direction of an efficient distribution of the internal secretions and sexual energies to the general physical and mental organism. These three several principles of the practice of Regeneration we shall now ask you to consider in detail.

I. The Production of Regenerative Power.
In the lower animal kingdom, Nature employs
the subconscious or unconscious mentality of
the creatures in the production of both the
generative cells and the regenerative secretions
and energies, at the appropriate times and in
the normal quantities, without any interfer-
ence or assistance from the conscious mentality. But man, here as elsewhere, pays the
price of the evolution of his conscious mentality while also reaping the benefits.

In many different ways man has consciously
interfered with the normal and regular operations of his subconscious mind, and as a result
he has brought on more or less abnormal physical conditions which are unknown among the
lower animals. For ages he has suffered more
or less by reason of this; the higher he has
mounted the ladder of conscious mentality the
more has he interfered with the natural, instinctive operations of the subconscious mentality presiding over his physical functions.

Of course, Nature has managed to overcome
this difficulty to a considerable extent by the
exercise of her seemingly boundless ingenuity,
but in spite of this man has managed to throw
many obstacles in the path of Nature—he has
poured sand into Natures oil-cups, and has
thrown scrap-iron into delicate parts of her
intricate machinery. The study of Psycho-
Therapy, Suggestion, and the general subject

of the Influence of Mental States upon Physical
Conditions will furnish countless illustrations
of the above stated general principle.

But, here as elsewhere, a still higher knowl-.
edge is now tending to lead man out of this
unfortunate condition, and in the end he will
be all the better for his employment of his
conscious mind in reference to his physical
processes. This, because he is now learning
that just as the conscious mind may interfere
with the normal processes of the subconscious
mentality presiding over the physical functions,
so it may be employed to aid and encourage
this subconscious mentality in its beneficent
vital activities. The wonderful results of the
various forms of Mental Healing afford an
illustration of this fact; and every dav men are
learning that the right kind of mental states
will not only bring about a restoration of
health but will also preserve, maintain and
promote the normal condition of health.

Man in his original and primitive state was
like any of the higher animals in his employment of his sexual powers. He used these
powers solely for the purpose of reproduction,
in response to the instinctive urge, and was
governed by the instinctive promptings of the
female of the species, as are all the higher animals; the sexual act normally being performed
only at certain periods determined by the in-

stincts of the female, and being refrained from during the period of gestation and nursing.

As man evolved in conscious mentality he began to cultivate deliberately his sex indulgences, and to exercise his sex powers in a manner and to an extent unknown to the higher animals. There is no higher animal which violates the natural, instinctive sex rules as does man. Man has developed the habit of sex indulgence in and out of season, and in direct contradiction to the normal promptings of the female nature. He has developed race habits which have became "second nature." He has broken down the instinct which causes the female animal to repulse the advances of the male at all times except those of the mating period, and which causes the male animal to evince no interest in the sexual activities while the female is pregnant or while she is nursing her young.

In short, man has gradually transformed the sexual activities from their natural manifestation of reproduction into their abnormal manifestation of a regular, oft-repeated, physical performance which affords satisfying sensations. He has deliberately taken the sexual appetite, just as he has taken the other physical appetites, away from the simple, natural, normal plane of manifestation.

This habit has been strengthened during the long history of the race, until at the present

time the natural and normal purpose of the
sexual organism has been lost sight of; the
latter is now regarded as designed primarily
for the purposes of pleasurable indulgence, its
energies are artificially stimulated by the imagination and general thought on the subject,
and its powers are recklessly wasted and dissipated in over-indulgence and excess. This, of
course, is equally true of the functions of eating
and drinking, for these also were designed by
Nature for certain definite and simple purposes,
but have now become perverted into sense-
gratification which too often is carried to almost insane excesses.

On the other hand, the mind of man has
suffered from a reaction from the above-stated
perversion of the original sex nature. Just as
many men have made a god of sex-indulgence,
and have bowed down before it and worshipped
at its shrine, so have other men made a devil
of it, and now speak and think of it as a ma-
lignant thing—a tempting demon to be feared
and hated. This reaction has resulted in a
decided perversion, namely that which has
caused men to regard Sex as essentially evil,
and as a work of the tempting, evil spirit in
man's nature.

Even those indulging in sexual excesses frequently speak of Sex in the coarsest, most abu-
sive terms, and manifest an evident contempt
for it even while making a god (or a devil) of

it. Many who admit the power of Sex over them, and who make a habit of excessive sexual indulgence, frankly admit that they consider it "a necessary evil," and feel inclined to apologize for its existence and its power over them. Many, at least tacitly, seem to regard Sex as akin to a drug-habit which, privately indulged in, excessively and often harmfully, is to be detested, abused and apologized for in public.

These two mental attitudes toward Sex, resulting from the action of and reaction from the perverted habits of the race which are so far removed from the evident intentions and purposes of Nature, have resulted in two strong, but opposite, general classes of mental states concerning thoughts, ideas, and mental pictures toward Sex.

On the one hand is the conscious mental attitude which is reflected in the subconscious mentality and which results in the active stimulation of the sexual nature for the purposes of sexual indulgence. This attitude, in its extreme form, results in the employment of every means of mental and emotional excitation of the sexual energies to the end of enabling the individual to manifest sexual activity frequently and repeatedly—this ability being mistaken for "sexual power," and as something to be sought for and encouraged. This is clearly contrary to Nature.

On the other hand, there is the mental attitude which regards Sex as an evil, impure thing, all thoughts of which are to be resisted, inhibited and repressed so far as is possible— in this view Sex is regarded as a devilish device designed to trap the unwary and to lead them to perdition. As all modern psychologists and physiologists know, this perverted mental attitude really defeats its own object, and in the end brings on either more or less of sexual perversion or else occasional reactions in which the individual falls a victim to the, to him, devilish devices from which he is seeking to escape—the reaction carrying him to the other extreme.

Careful thinkers have seen that the escape from these two extremes of wrong-views is to be found only in that universal panacea—the Golden Mean between the two extremes. In this case the Golden Mean is the mental attitude of viewing Sex as just what it is in Nature's eyes and mind, i. e., a natural, normal, clean, pure, physical process of reproduction of the species, proper and good in its right time and place, but neither a god to be worshiped nor yet a devil to be feared and dreaded. If men were to think and speak of Sex just as of any other natural function, then all the mystery would fall from it, and also all the exaggerated worship of it on one hand and the exaggerated fear and dread of it on the other hand. There is a great need of a mighty Teacher who will cast out from the Temple of Sex these false leering gods and grinning devils.

The understanding of the scientific principles of Regeneration will do much toward bringing about in the individual a sane mental balance concerning Sex. This sane balance and knowledge will set into operation and activity the natural powers of the sexual organism whereby the regenerative secretions are produced.

When the mind clearly perceives that the sexual organism has as one of its purposes the secretion of certain powerful substances containing energies which will produce mental and physical invigoration, energy and power, and that this energy is largely dissipated by the sexual excesses of the average individual, then will it gradually adjust itself to this new view, and will employ its subconscious powers in that direction rather than in the old way.

The new need being recognized, the subconscious mentality will proceed to supply it; the old need being seen to have been exaggerated, the subconscious mentality will no longer over-supply it, but will limit its supply to normal and natural proportions. A new, proper, normal and natural balance will be established, and the old, abnormal, "lop-sided' adjustment will be replaced by the normal, well-balanced equipoise.

Likewise, this new and sane mental attitude toward Sex will do away with the perverted conception of Sex as an unclean, impure element of human nature. When it is perceived that Sex is essentially pure and worthy, and that all of "evil" connected with it arises from artificial, unnatural excesses and habits, then will cease that forced repression of all thoughts concerning the sexual nature, which repression is so often accompanied by or followed by the reaction to the other extreme. Just as the knowledge of the Truth is followed by the casting out of the false gods and hideous idols of Sex Worship, so is that knowledge followed by the casting out of the images of the devils and demons of Sex Revilement. As the ancient proverb said: "When the true gods arrive, the false gods and devils disappear."

All this brings us up to the question of "The Production of Regenerative Power," or the means of "The normal production of the internal secretions of the genital glands for the purpose of physical and mental reinvigoration, recuperation and revitalization." We might devote many pages of detailed description of methods designed for this important purpose, but at the end the essence of the idea would be found to be contained in one paragraph, as follows:

Fix in your mind the clear, strong, definite idea or mental picture of the secretion of the

Regenerative Substances by the Genital Glands, and add to the idea or picture the details of the purpose and certain effect of such secretions upon the entire mental and physical system. So far as possible, visualize the production of these regenerative elements, and the concentrated power latent within them. Desire earnestly and ardently that your organism shall secrete these substances in sufficient amount, and with sufficient power, to effect the results wished by you. Confidently expect that Nature will perform this work for you, through the processes of the subconscious mentality and the mechanism of the sexual organism. And, finally, set your will into operation with determination—persistently will that your subconscious mentality and your physical organism shall operate along the lines which you have clearly and strongly pictured, idealized and visualized, which you confidently expect to be actualized, and which you are now willing into operation. If you do this, Nature will do the rest.

Finally, do not permit yourself to be deluded by the teachings of certain mistaken teachers of Regeneration, and their followers, who hold 'that in order to produce a full secretion of Regenerative Power it is necessary, or at least advisable, to direct the thought and imagination toward amatory subjects or exciting images for the purpose of stimulating the sexual glands to additional secretion. Not only is this unnecessary, but it is positively contrary to the spirit of the true teachings of Regeneration; and the practice of such methods tend to produce results diametrically opposed to those of Regeneration.

We warn you positively against any such teachings and the methods based upon the same. Instead of "holding the thought" of sexually exciting things, you should hold the mind firmly and steadily upon the regenerative offices of the sexual- organism—its re-generative functions, not its generative ones. The ideal should be that of Conservation and Regeneration, not of indulgence, dissipation and the thoughts and objects leading up to them. We expressly caution you to use wise discrimination in this matter, and to beware of this wolf-teaching disguised in the garments of the Truth.

In the psychological principles and methods outlined in the single paragraph of instruction given a little further back you will find all that is required in the way of instruction along these special lines. You will find in that paragraph a complete working theory of practice, and an efficient practical working method of employing that theory, the application of which will set into activity and operation the psychological forces concerned with the Production of Regenerative Power.

If you will set these psychological forces into operation, then Nature will operate through the subconscious mentality which presides over the physical organism, and will produce these secretions in sufficient amount and strength, just as by means of similar methods she secretes the necessary gastric and intestinal juices, the bile, etc. Unmarried men and women need have no fear that the practice of these psychological methods will impair their reproductive powers when they enter into the married state of life. On the contrary, they will be even still better fitted for these important offices, when the time for them arrives, by reason of their previous avoidance of waste and dissipation of their reproductive powers and the appropriate secretions.

In this method, your conscious mind is concerned merely with the furnishing of the design, plan, mold, or pattern of that which you wish to be materialized or actualized—your subconscious mentality attends to the details of the process in its own special way. This is the same psychological principle which operates in all cases of Mental Healing, and in all instances of the Influence of Mind over Body. In it are called into action the three great psychological principles of Idealization, Visualization and Actualizaton. In it are manifested the great powers of "Definite Ideals, Insistent Desire, Confident Expectation and Persistent

Determination." If you will practice this method you will soon have actual proof of its effective performance, for you will experience the increased energy and power resulting from its, employment.

II. **Sane and Rational Sexual Temperance.** The excessive use, or rather the abuse, of the sexual organism in the direction of sexual indulgence is logically followed by the depletion of the regenerative powers of the general system, as well as by the waste which arises by reason of the diversion to the reproductive organism of the vital energy which Nature intends also to be distributed to the other organs, glands and centres of the system. The individual who wastes or dissipates his or her sexual energies inevitably draws upon Nature's reserve forces intended for other purposes, and at the same time diverts from its legitimate channels the regenerative energies which Nature has provided for the invigoration, strengthening and vitalization of the whole system.

Wisdom plainly dictates a change in this respect. One who gives serious thought to the subject cannot well escape becoming impressed with the need of a hardy temperance in the employment of these important energies and secreted substances. The theory is plain, but the actual practice and application is soon perceived to be fraught with difficulties. Many of the teachers along the lines of Regeneration

have failed by reason of their too radical and
too extreme teachings concerning the methods
to be employed, and the too rigid and inelastic
rules laid down by them for the guidance of
their followers.

Such teachers have overlooked, or else have
deliberately ignored, the fact that many generations of excessive use or abuse of the sexual
powers have resulted in the establishment of
race-habits which have become firmly rooted
in the race-consciousness, and which are most
difficult to overcome. Attempts to observe
faithfully such rules have often been followed
by a natural reaction in which the whole idea
has been rejected as impractical, impracticable
and contrary to human nature.

Strictly speaking, it may be stated that the
only legitimate purpose of the sexual relations
between the sexes is that of reproduction; and
that, accordingly, all other employment of
them is illegitimate and abnormal. But, in
view of the acquired habits of the race which
are manifested in the marital relations of most
individuals, attempts to confine the sexual relation to such comparatively infrequent exercise of the sexual powers have proved most
difficult, and efforts in this direction have met
with failure. Here, again, the Golden Mean
must be sought. Fanaticism, extreme methods
and rules, and similar courses are, therefore, to

be avoided, and practical wisdom must be established and maintained.

For this reason, we shall not attempt to lay down positive, set, cut-and-dried, inflexible, rules governing this matter. Instead, we shall content ourselves with urging our students to endeavor to use moderation, temperance, and normal self-restraint in their practice of Regeneration. We feel well satisfied in adopting this idea of the Golden Mean by reason of our knowledge that the individual who acquires a clear and full knowledge of the principles of Regeneration as set forth in this book will instinctively, subconsciously and almost automatically begin gradually to exercise such moderation, temperance and rational restraint in the case, without the severe struggle which usually follows the attempt to employ the extreme methods and rules laid down by the radical, extreme and sometimes fanatical teaching along these lines.

Knowledge usually operates to modify even the subconscious actions which are opposed to the known Truth. There is a great fact embodied in the statement that "the Truth shall set you free." The knowledge of the truths concerning Regeneration will gradually filter down from the conscious to the subconscious mentality, and the latter will proceed to modify, tone down and bring to normal condition the desires which lead to such action.

The desire and will to exercise the powers of Regeneration will tend to modify, neutralize and inhibit the will and desire to abuse the sexual powers and to dissipate their energies.

An old story of George Fox, the founder of the Society of Friends (commonly known as the Quakers) will illustrate this psychological principle. The story relates that an ardent and extreme Quaker complained to Fox that William Penn, recently converted to Quakerism, persisted in wearing his sword; the wearing of weapons being opposed to the teachings and rules of the Friends. The complaining Quaker wished Fox to command Penn to discard his sword, or else to expel him from the Society. Fox, however, being well versed in human psychology, said: "Nay, let Friend William wear his sword so long as he feels a desire to do so; when the time comes for him to discard it, he will no longer wish to wear it!" Time proved the wisdom of Fox, for Penn eventually found within himself such a distaste for the wearing of a sword that, without commands, he discarded it. Had he been commanded to drop the sword before his inner consciousness dictated it, he would probably have rebelled and withdrawn from the Society.

And so, in the case before us, it usually will be found that the knowledge of the Truth, seeping into the inner consciousness and filtering down to the subconscious mentality, will cause the disappearance of the acquired, abnormal race-habits, and will bring the desire and will of the individual back to the normal standard. In the same way, the same causes will operate to remove the abnormal dread, fear and hatred of Sex from the minds of those who have entertained these feelings, and will thus remove the peril of the dangerous reactions from such mental attitude which we have noted, and will bring the individual back to the normal standard of a sane mental attitude toward Sex, with its inevitable accompaniment of temperance, moderation and desirable restraint and control.

In this connection we would add that the habit and practice of directing the sexual energy to the general system, in the method of Regeneration, will strongly tend to inhibit and neutralize the inordinate sexual cravings and urges toward indulgence which have rendered the practice of sexual temperance and moderation so difficult for so many persons. The diffusion of the sexual energies in this general direction will be found to relieve the localized pressure toward manifestation in sexual indulgence, and will serve to free the individual from the tyrant desires which in the past have led him astray from the path of wisdom, and often from the path of duty and morality. The transmutation of the sexual energy into mental and physical energy works a tremendous change in the nature and character of the struggle with the old acquired race-habits: this fact is attested to by thousands who have undergone this experience. At the same time, the ability to employ the sexual energy for the purposes of procreation is not affected or impaired.

Here is the General Rule: Strive for the Golden Mean; exercise moderation, temperance and self-control; strive to transmute the impulse into creative energy along the lines of mental and physical creative work; and remember always that, in the end, the Truth will set you free.

The subject of the Practice of Regeneration will be considered further in the following section of this book.

X

TRANSMUTATION

In the preceding section of this book you have considered the two phases of the practice of Regeneration known, respectively, as the Production of Regenerative Power, and the exercise of Sane and Rational Temperance in the use of the sexual energies in their primary offices. In the present section we shall ask you to consider the third phase of the Practice of Regeneration, namely, that phase known as the Direction of the Transmuted Sexual Energy.

III. **The Direction of the Transmuted Sexual Energy.** We have now reached that point in our inquiry and instruction concerned with the important subject of the employment of the psychological powers in the direction of an efficient distribution of the internal secretions and sexual energies to the general physical and mental organism. To this final end all the teaching and methods of Regeneration tend.

Here, as in the case of the normal production of these secretions and energies, we find that the essence of the methods to be employed may be condensed into a few sentences. The details of the practice must be left to the exercise of the judgment and common sense of the individual, but there is but little if any danger of his going astray in the matter once he has fixed in his mind the fundamental, basic essential principles. These fundamental and basic essential principles in the present case may be stated as follows:

Form in your mind the clear, definite, positive idea or mental picture of the presence within the Genital Glands of an abundant supply of the concentrated, potent Regenerative Power. Employ your ideative and imagining faculties to create a positive, clear and strong idea or mental image of the presence within you of such potent energies inherent in the internal secretions of the Genital Glands. At the same time cultivate the firm conviction and belief that these potent energies are capable of regenerating, reinvigorating and strengthening the entire physical and mental organism, or any part of it to which they may be specially directed by you; and, above all, endeavor to enter into a full recognition and realization of your power to so direct these energies to the parts of your organism selected by you, just as you would direct a stream of electrictiy or magnetism under your control and direction.

At the same time, you should awaken within yourself the strong, insistent desire and wish that these potent energies will flow under your direction, and according to your concentrated will, proceeding to the regions of your organism which you have selected for the purpose of Regeneration. This insistent desire is an important basis for the exercise of the persistent will. Finally, you should firmly, determinedly and persistently employ your will toward the end that these energies may flow freely when and where you may direct them, this direction being supplied by your mental picture or strong idea which serves as the chart, map, pattern, or mold for the actualization or materialization of the process.

In directing the flow of the Regenerative Power to any part of your physical or mental organism, you should first form the mental pattern, chart, or mold, which you desire to be followed in the actualization process. You must also actually "see" (mentally) the flow of the power to the parts, glands, or centres indicated in your mental chart or pattern. The more clearly you can visualize the process, the more effective will be the result. After you have practiced the method of Regeneration for a short time, this visualization and conscious use of the directing will will become practically instinctive and automatic, the subconscious mentality having taken over the process as a habit, just as it does any action which you practice or perform frequently.

You may either "treat" your entire system in this way, or else you may direct the flow of power to any particular part, portion, or centre of your body which you may feel to require or

likely to be specially benefited by the reinvigoration and strengthening.   However, even
when you treat special parts of the body in this
way, it is well to conclude the treatment by
a general treatment in which you "flush" or
saturate the whole body with a supply of the
reinvigorating power.

For increased mental power and activity, the
current is to be directed to the brain; for increased breathing power, to the lungs; for increased muscular power, to the muscles in
question; for increased digestive power, to the
stomach and intestines; and so on, each organ
or part receiving its special treatment.

Many have found it helpful to employ the
rhythmic breathing method in connection with
this process of directing the flow of the Regenerative Power.   This method is simple: it consists
merely of slow, deep, regular breathing, in slow
measured rhythm or "regular time." With each
inhalation you should visualize the rise of the Regenerative Power to the Solar Plexus (in the
region of the "pit of the stomach"), and with
each exhalation you should visualize the outward
flow (upward or downward, or both, as the case
may be) of the Regenerative Power to the selected parts of the body, or to the body as a whole.
This produces what may be called a psychological
"pumping" process which is reproduced in actualization by the rise and distribution of the Regenerative Power.   A certain "knack" is required

here, but a little practice soon produces this—the process is quite easy of performance.

You will find this method to be extremely helpful when employed at times when you are tired, fatigued, or overworked; also when you may feel depressed, despondent or "blue." It seems to "pump new life into one," as an enthusiastic practicer of the method once expressed it. It acts to stimulate the circulation, to "clean out" the nerve-channels, to vitalize the brain, and to stimulate, reinvigorate and energize the entire system. In many cases it produces the feeling, and the subsequent outward manifestation, of youthfulness of spirit. Indeed, the ancients were quite justified in figuratively styling it "The Elixir of Life," or "The Fountain of Youth." Its enthusiastic followers, ancient and modern, attribute to it all of the actual benefits which are reported as following the surgical "gland transplantation" which we have noted in preceding sections of this book.

The unmarried man or woman may employ this method with excellent results when he or she experiences the rise of exciting amatory or sexual feelings which in many cases may cause physical or mental strain or distress. In such cases there is experienced a decided and positive "relief"— the tension is withdrawn—when this method is employed; moreover, the sexual energy is in such case actually transmuted into Regenerative Power and is employed for the upbuilding and strengthening of body and mind. If young persons of both sexes knew of this method, there would be fewer cases of their "going wrong" because of their sexual passions. Instead of a forced repression, under a nervous strain and tension, there would be secured the relief of transmutation and diffusion of these potent energies of the system, and health and vigor would replace nervous strain and the strenuous effort of repression.

If the moralists would teach this method and principle in connection with their general precepts, their task would be rendered easier and far more successful. There is a great field open here for workers along the lines of "social purity" and similar movements. There is a far greater force in a positive "do," than in a negative "don't." Here, indeed, is "the way out" for persons whose sexual natures assert themselves too strongly, and who wish to lead a chaste, moral, sexual life although beset by the temptations which arise on all sides. Here is a method of practical "morality,' in keeping with the highest precepts of religion, duty, and social rectitude. Those interested in the moral welfare of the race would do well to consider carefully and seriously the principles of Regeneration.

The effect of the Regenerative Power is especially noticable when the individual is employed in "creative" work along material or mental lines. The Regenerative Power, being essentially "creative," acts with special force when the hands or head are employed in work which manifests in inventing, designing, construction, building-up, putting together—in short, in "creative work" in general. One may create mentally, materially, on many planes, as well as on the procreative plane of manifestation. Writers, inventors, designers, teachers, artisans, architects, and many others performing constructive, creative work, may be greatly benefited by the methods of Regeneration. Here is another valuable hint: in fact, the study of Regenerative Power and Regeneration is filled with valuable and suggestive hints which may be taken up and applied to advantage by those wise enough to perceive and appreciate them.

In addition to the physical and mental improvement manifested by those practicing the methods of Regeneration, there is another phase of development which has attracted the attention of careful students of this subject, and which should be mentioned here. We allude to that subtle, powerful "something" which is known as "personal magnetism"—this is well known in actual experience, although it is subtle and so elusive that it is most difficult to describe. It may be said to consist of that peculiar personal "charm" which some persons have, and which others seem to lack.

Persons who are "strongly sexed" frequently display this power in higher or lower forms and phases; this has caused some writers to suppose that it is intimately related to the sexual nature, and to suggest the development of the latter as a means of cultivating the power. But this view is but a half-truth, and a dangerous half-truth at that. It is not necessary for one to develop the ordinary procreative sexual power in order to become "magnetic"; rather should one endeavor to master the principles and methods of Regeneration as the road to such power.

The person who succeeds in transmuting the sexual energy, and in diffusing it to all the physical and emotional centres of his system, becomes highly "magnetic"—highly charged with "personal magnetism," in many cases. Here, then, is a safe, moral and efficacious method, which may be approved of by the most conservative moralist, and which is free from the glaring faults and dangerous elements of the "strongly sexed" teachings. Moreover, the "magnetism" generated by this method is clean, wholesome, and exalting, and far removed from the impure, harmful, lowering influence too often present in the "magnetism" of persons of the "highly sexed" type who live lives too often far from desirable, beneficial, moral, or righteous.

In this connection we wish to call your attention to a fact which has been noted and commented upon by many careful students of the subject of Regeneration, and which has greatly puzzled many good people. We allude to the fact that persons practicing the methods of Regeneration, and who live according to its principles, seem to possess a potent quality of attraction for persons of the other sex; in many cases such attraction and its results proving embarrassing and in the nature of a temptation. The explanation' of this fact is found in the Law of Polarity which is found manifest in all natural activities; we shall not go into details concerning this law, but merely wish to indicate the nature of the explanation. The person understanding the principles and methods of Personal Power will have no difficulty in meeting successfully these results of his attracting power.

Concerning this attractive influence, the following comments of Dr. Hiram E. Butler, may prove interesting and instructive. Dr. Butler, a lifelong and earnest investigator and teacher of the principles of Regeneration, though perhaps somewhat of an extremist in his views and methods, says:

"Those following these methods will have all the bloom of health, and in addition will possess that personal magnetism which is so attractive, and which is really one of the strongest factors of success even in a business way; it is, in fact, the main requisite for the success of speakers, teachers, lawyers, doctors and salesmen. We have often heard that those who are living this life have added power of attracting the opposite sex. Now, here lies one of the greatest dangers—that of attracting to oneself those who will use every means to ensnare one. Young people who live

this life become possessed of such attractive powers that they usually have their choice of a com-
panion from any class of life. This, however, is
the least important consideration."

Dr. Butler also says: "We know that it is an
impossibility to express in words one-half that is
to be attained through this mode of life; but we
will mention a few facts and leave you to prove
them by experience; then you will know for yourself. It gives a joyous happy feeling to body and
mind: clears up the intellect so that one may
readily understand the most abstruse subjects; it
gives strength and decision of character and directness of purpose; a love of refinement, purity,
goodness, honor, justice and morality; in every
conceivable direction it adds to the capacity of
mind and body; a process of growth which will
steadily continue; we have never known anyone
who could define the limits of the possibility of
increase; we have known some of the most marvelous mind-powers gained through living the
regenerate life; we have seen young men and
women with pale faces, dim eyes, and poor health,
begin a course of lessons on this subject, but before the course closed inside of three weeks, their
eyes would grow bright and the color would return to their cheeks."

In addition to the physical and mental benefits
resulting from the knowledge and practice of the
principles and methods of Regeneration, there are
spiritual benefits to be derived from them. The

awakening of the mind and soul to the true nature
and character of the Principle of Sex is akin to
the admission of Light to the dark chambers of
the soul, this radiance serving to drive out many,
slimy, crawling, loathsome creatures which have
been making their home there. Chief among these
loathsome creatures are those twin-devils known,
respectively as "Abuse of Sex," and "Fear and
Hatred of Sex."

When the Sex Principle of Nature is seen to
be that which it really is, namely clean, pure,
normal, righteous, then the mind and soul cease
to abuse and lower it by excesses, wrong uses,
abuses and dissipation of its energies; and, at the
same time, all fear of its evil power, or the perverted and abnormal hatred of its principle, perish. The recognition, realization and manifestation of the principles of Regeneration open a new
world of spiritual life and living, just as they
have unfolded a new world of mental and physical
life and living.

With the realization that Sex is no devil, no
tempting demon, no monster of evil, but is instead
a clean, pure, righteous natural principle, then
does the world seem to brighten and the clouds
of distrust melt away. Then perishes the harmful conception of a world which is half-right and
half-wrong; and there dawns a vision of a world
of Righteousness, in which Evil is but the shadow
of Good—the results of Good misunderstood and
misapplied, wrongfully, misused instead of righte-

ously used. Then, perhaps, more of us may feel that we can say with a clear consciousness of Truth that "God is in His Heaven, and all's right with the World!"

We trust that in this book we have given you a new insight into this highly important, though greatly misunderstood, subject of Regenerative Power and Regeneration. The subject has been so misrepresented both by its opponents and also its over-zealous and fanatical friends that it seems to be time that a sane, rational, conservative presentatior of the Golden Mean of its teachings, its principles, and its methods, should be made.

We realize that we have but "scratched the surface" of this great and rich field of thought and practice, but we trust that we have at least directed to that field the earnest attention and careful thought of many who, otherwise, would have remained in ignorance of its existence, or who, perhaps, would have avoided it by reason of previously acquired misconceptions concerning it.

In conclusion, let us remind you of that axiom of Regeneration which states that: "That which brought you into being, will continue you in being; that which created you, will re-create you; that which generated you, will regenerate you; that which breathed Life into you, will continue to breathe Life into you if you will but set its power into activity."

* * * * * * * *

The Master Formula

In the application of the principles, and in the practice of the methods upon which this instruction is based, you will be greatly helped by the careful study and the faithful observance of the spirit of the Master Formula of Attainment which is frequently referred to in the series of books of which the present volume is one.

The Master Formula of Attainment is as follows: "(1) Definite Ideals; (2) Insistent Desire; (3) Confident Expectation; (4) Persistent Determination (5) Balanced Compensation." Reduced to popular terms, it is as follows: "You may have anything you want, provided that you (1) know exactly what you want, (2) want it hard enough, (3) confidently expect to obtain it, (4) persistently determine to obtain it, and (5) are willing to pay the price of its attainment."

FINIS

COSIMO is a specialty publisher of books and publications that inspire, inform, and engage readers. Our mission is to offer unique books to niche audiences around the world.

COSIMO BOOKS publishes books and publications for innovative authors, nonprofit organizations, and businesses. **COSIMO BOOKS** specializes in bringing books back into print, publishing new books quickly and effectively, and making these publications available to readers around the world.

COSIMO CLASSICS offers a collection of distinctive titles by the great authors and thinkers throughout the ages. At **COSIMO CLASSICS** timeless works find new life as affordable books, covering a variety of subjects including: Business, Economics, History, Personal Development, Philosophy, Religion & Spirituality, and much more!

COSIMO REPORTS publishes public reports that affect your world, from global trends to the economy, and from health to geopolitics.

FOR MORE INFORMATION CONTACT US AT
INFO@COSIMOBOOKS.COM

➢ if you are a book lover interested in our current catalog of books

➢ if you represent a bookstore, book club, or anyone else interested in special discounts for bulk purchases

➢ if you are an author who wants to get published

➢ if you represent an organization or business seeking to publish books and other publications for your members, donors, or customers.

**COSIMO BOOKS ARE ALWAYS
AVAILABLE AT ONLINE BOOKSTORES**

**VISIT COSIMOBOOKS.COM
BE INSPIRED, BE INFORMED**